# Find Your Brave

### Embrace Fear as A Gift
### To Show Up, Shine and Succeed

## Jackie Capers-Brown

Copyright © 2018 Jackie Capers-Brown

Cover design: Pro_ebookcovers by Angie on Fiverr.com

Originally published in the United States of America by Slay Your Greatness Academy.

All rights reserved including the right to reproduce this book or portions thereof in any form whatsoever without written permission except in the case of brief quotations embodied in critical articles and reviews.

For permission and information about special discounts for bulk purchases, please contact Jackie Capers-Brown, c/o Slay Your Greatness Academy Subsidiary Rights Department at www.jackiecapersbrown.com

**Disclaimer:** The author of this book does not dispense medical advice or prescribe the use of any techniques as a form of treatment for physical, emotional, or medical problems.without the advice of a physician either directly or indirectly. The intent of the information shared in this book is only to offer information of a general nature to help you in your quest towards self-development goals. In the event that you use any of the information in this book for yourself, the author and publisher assume no responsibility for your actions or results.

ISBN - 13: 978-1727460438
ISBN - 10: 172746043x


Revised Edition September, 2019

# Dedication

*For my teachers, school administrators and all the other adults working at Carver Elementary School in Columbia, SC from 1966 thru 1969*

*AND*

*The brave women and men I had the pleasure of working with during my award-winning corporate leadership career*

*Thank you for helping me think bigger, believe in my bold dreams and trust in my ability to achieve audacious goals.*

# Contents

Introduction, *page 7*

Part One: The Awakening, *page 19*

Practice 1  Dare to Desire, *page 59*
Practice 2  Embrace Your Authentic Self, *page 87*
Practice 3  You Are Enough, *page 103*

Part Two: The Alignment, *page 131*

Practice 4  Show Up for Yourself, *page 139*
Practice 5  Disrupt Your Limits , *page 145*
Practice 6  Transcending Fear, *page 151*

Part Three: The Ascension, *page 171*
Practice 7   Be Driven by Discovery, *page 179*
Practice 8   Brave the Way Forward, *page 193*

Notes, *page 204*

About the Author, *page 206*

# Disclaimers + Admissions

**This book will help you reclaim the brave you were born with.** The book encourages, equips and empowers you to create and experience a paradigm shift about fear. It shares practices that will help you reconnect to your authentic voice and spiritual authority, while embracing the truth of your enoughness. The wisdom shared will shift how you see, feel, think and relate to your fears.

1. **You cannot live your best life seeking to be someone you are not wired to be.** You can become more of who you were born to be.

2. **I believe there is nothing more powerful than a soul on fire inspired to embody and express unconditional love.** Unconditional love toward yourself and others will always be an antidote to fear.

3. **I admit that fear is not an emotion you will completely banish from your life.** But, you can learn how to transform your relationship with fear. You can start to embrace fear as a gift to show up as your authentic self, shine the light of your brilliance and succeed in life on your terms.

4. **I am a champion of greatness.** I encourage you to believe you are worthy of experiencing the abundant life that's available to you. Trust in your ability to discern what's true and best for you. This moment is calling you to become the bravest version of your authentic self.

*Brave the Way,*
*Jackie Capers-Brown*

*Scared is what you're feeling.*

*Brave is what you're doing.*

**~ Emma Donoghue**

# Introduction

*Find Your Brave* is the endless practice of embracing fear as a gift that represents a door we must open and walk through to 'level up' our capacity to realize our great potential. This adventure will challenge you to show up in the fullness of your authentic power and spiritual authority to be of service and add value in the lives of others in your unique way. The fundamentals of this process is, an open mind, an open and courageous heart, childlike faith, a beginner's mind, and an obsession for personal freedom. These were once our natural states of BEing before we began to be hypnotized into believing *more* in the messages of fear than the messages of hope, love, faith, generosity, compassion and courage.

Because you have been inundated with so many fear-based messages during the course of your life, you have been led to believe your fear-based thinking is natural.

The freedom you seek from your fear-based thinking depends on your receptivity to the idea that your point of power to change how you relate to fear is always in the present moment. *Regardless of what you have been led to believe about fear, you can learn new ways to relating to fear.*

The brave act of considering this possibility challenges our perception about the meanings we have associated with fear. It questions how we have allowed our fears to shape our individual and collective identity. It disrupts the fear-induced assumptions we have believed about ourselves, others, and the world. Our commitment to learn and implement best practices that can help us reframe and relate to fear from an empowering perspective will liberate our soul and allow it to experience the freedom it craves.

You are all too familiar with how your fear-based thinking has created internal barriers to the breakthroughs you believe will 'level up' your life. You are ready and willing to learn what it takes to relate to fear differently. You have chosen to surrender to the inspired unction within your soul for a greater sense of freedom by purchasing a copy of *Find Your Brave. Thank you. I will honor your time, energy and resources.*

This is a defining moment in your life. It indicates that you are ready to believe bigger, feel freer, and be bolder toward manifesting new possibilities in your life. You are open to learning what it takes to realize your great potential. I applaud your initiative to champion your potential.

This intention will be achieved through the application of the *Brave the Way* practices outlined in this book. This journey to *Find Your Brave* is a pilgrimage of the heart. You may have thought that the freedom you seek from your fear-based thinking is solely about learning practices and strategies that help you DO things different. That is part of the process. However, much of this journey is about how you relate to fear. In other words, how you are BEing when you face a fear during your life's journey. BEing different toward a fear requires a shift in the way that you relate to it. Like most successful personal development practices, this is an inside-out process.

This process starts with making peace with yourself, and the fear you believe has been holding you back from leveling up some aspect of your life. Cultivating a heart space of acceptance toward "what is" will help you be open to seeing yourself and fear with new eyes of understanding. When you are open to seeing fear differently, you are receptive to the idea that you can feel differently about it. As a result, you will respond differently to it. These perspective shifts will help you to focus your energy and attention toward taking new actions, even while you are afraid, to manifest new possibilities in your life.

Whenever you attempt to ignore, dismiss, or numb yourself to avoid dealing with fear, (or any other emotion) your free will is subject to be imprisoned by invisible shackles in your mind and heart. This state of BEing keeps you running scared and denying the truth and power of your authentic self. This state of BEing torments your soul with needless suffering.

Your authentic self craves freedom. It doesn't crave conformity to the status quo. It wants you to discover the full power of who you are to live with purpose and soar to new heights in life.

My distorted thoughts and beliefs about fear, and the breakthroughs experienced after facing my greatest fear: the unexpected loss of my son Blease ushered me onto this adventure for my soul. Today, I strive to deepen my understanding about how the tsunami of fear-based messages we ingest on a regular basis in our culture influences what we believe, what we feel, and what we do in every aspect of our life. Far too many people are suffering in silence because they are imprisoned by fear-based thoughts and beliefs. If that resonates with you, just know, I understand.

## Benefits and Costs Related to Fear

Life has dealt me hands which allowed me to experience the euphoria that comes when my mind, body and spirit feels free and unencumbered by fear. I know what it feels like to believe in the limitless power of the Holy Spirit working in and through me to overcome daunting circumstances, and achieve goals that were deemed impossible to accomplish by someone like me.

Life has also dealt me hands which allowed me to experience seasons when fear-based thinking and beliefs shackled me into self-made prisons. During each of these experiences, my way of thinking and BEing resulted in me living below my potential and disconnected from my authentic self and spiritual authority in Christ.

Regardless of how many fears I have been able to transcend, I have accepted that embracing fear as a gift is an endless practice. Why? Because as long as I live and strive to grow and flourish, life is going to require me to face the unknown and unfamiliar fears.

This knowing motivates me to maintain daily, weekly, and monthly rituals that keep me grounded in my faith and spiritual authority, as I strategically actualize what I believe to be God's plan for my life.

When I'm not grounded in the power of my spiritual authority, and I'm not open to making peace with myself and whatever fear I am being asked by life to transcend, my awareness and understanding is often distorted by a lack of clarity and feelings of powerlessness toward creating the change I want to experience.

I feel weak and constrained. I start to doubt myself which erodes my self-trust and inner sense of security. My inner-drive and motivation starts to diminish. I allow myself to be influenced by people whose mind and heart is dominated by doubt, worry and anxiety. I am not as diligent toward protecting my mind and heart from the fear-based messages that are widespread in our culture. Can you relate?

This ebb and flow between our fears and doubts, and our faith and trust is a reflection of our humanity. The resilience in our spirit helps us to face each day unsure of how it will actually unfold. We go about our day doing what is necessary to keep our lives in forward motion. It is our willingness to approach life and ourselves with radical acceptance that grants us access to the reservoir of strength in our spirit. We become curious. We become more creative. Our soul becomes lit with desires for new possibilities.

These states of BEing serve as evidence that there are treasures of insight, wisdom, and strength within us we have yet to discover. It is important that we bring them to the forefront of our consciousness to use in our quest to embrace fear as a gift and allow our authentic self to dominate how we show up in life.

We may not always remain conscious of this truth, but, each of us desire to live our life in close proximity to the rhythm of our authentic self. When we are the most aligned with our authentic self, we embody the energy of our bravest and boldest self. We nurture and nourish the faith, resolve, and emotional resiliency necessary to manage the inevitable struggles we face on our journey, while maintaining a steadfast assurance in our ability to achieve our dreams and goals.

The *Find Your Brave* process outlined in this book consists of eight *Brave the Way* practices that build upon each other to create a cohesive strategy that helps you devise a plan of action unique to who you are and your life situation. Each practice will help you gain the clarity to own the truth of your enoughness, seize new growth opportunities that empower you to level up your personal and professional success while having fun doing it.

**What You Can Expect**

I am honored to have the privilege to be your guide as you embark on this adventure to rediscover the power of your authentic self, and reclaim the brave you were born with.

## This book builds three central arguments:

- Your life story and experiences when viewed from the truth of your enoughness provide you with evidence that debunks any "I am not enough" narrative you may believe about yourself.
- Your acceptance of the legitimacy of your enoughness helps you develop and deepen your sense of self-trust. This state of BEing emboldens you with a certainty about your ability to handle life, and achieve audacious dreams and goals.
- You can learn how to relate to fear differently. It's a skill that will give you an advantage in many arenas. The foundation of this reality will be built on your willingness to become emotional interdependent, and develop the consciousness to see fear (not the physical danger kind of fear) as a gift that can fuel your growth, inspire you to redefine what is possible in your life, and soar to new heights in life.

The *Find Your Brave* process outlined in this book takes a mindfulness approach to transforming your relationship with fear. When you experience fundamental shifts in the way you see, feel and think about fear, each paradigm shift will transform the way you relate to fear. This shift in awareness will begin to embolden you to face your fears head on. It will expand your perspective and approach to fear. It will help to deepen your understanding of how embracing fear as a gift can enable you to evolve into the bravest version of your authentic self.

The *Brave the Way* practices shared in each chapter of this book reflect mindset, heart-set, and emotional interdependence skills which I believe are essential to becoming a fear-tamer. These practices will help you develop an empowering perspective about your ability to manage your fears as you brave your way forward and create new possibilities in your life.

Each practice serves as a compass to redirect your focus, energy, and effort toward an intended destination while walking boldly in your spiritual authority, authentic voice, and, in the truth of your enoughness. The effectiveness of each practice is dependent upon your ability to engage the fundamentals of developing and maintaining an open mind, an open and courageous heart, childlike faith, a beginner's mind, and ,an obsession for personal freedom.

In order for you to live your best life, you have to step into the arena as your authentic self to create the experiences you desire. Be encouraged by your efforts to show up for yourself in this moment. Life will show up for you with opportunities that will help you reach your intended destinations. Cultivate a healthy sense of self-trust and certainty about the truth of your enoughness. This mindset and heart space empowers your spiritual badassary.

Be proud of yourself. I am. Embarking on this journey is an act of bravery. Trusting yourself to do what it takes to embrace fear as a gift to show up, shine and succeed is an act of bravery. Believing that you are supported by Spirit to become your most powerful and authentic self is an act of bravery.

*Whatever you do, you need courage. Whatever course you decide upon, there is always someone to tell you that you are wrong. There are always difficulties arising that temp you to believe your critics are right.*

*To map out a course of action and follow it to an end requires some of the same courage that a soldier needs. Peace has its victories, but it takes brave men and women to win them."*

*~ Ralph Waldo Emerson*

# The Awakening

# Find Your Brave Process

The process is defined by the *Brave the Way* practices outlined in each chapter. It is designed to reconnect us with our authentic self and the truth of our enoughness while developing an empowering sense of self-trust. This internal state emboldens us to embrace fear as a gift that conveys wisdom that will support our efforts to create and live our best life.

### The Awakening

We make peace with ourselves. We acknowledge the truth of our fears. We embrace vulnerability as a super power to give our soul the freedom it craves. We become aware of how transforming the way we relate to fear begins with an awareness that fear is a heart matter. And what governs our heart defines our way of BEing.

### The Alignment

We honor the truth of our desires. Our authenticity distinguishes us as we show up for our dreams and disrupt conventional rules. We align with the energy of our authentic self to create experiences that are reflective of our dreams and desires.

### The Ascension

*Brave the Way practices become the dominate way we operate in our day-to-day life.* We believe in the truth of our enoughness. We embody a depth of self-trust that fuels our faith and inspires our heart with the courage and conviction to live bold and bloom.

One evening an elder Cherokee told his grandson about a battle that goes on inside all people. He said, "My son, the battle is between two wolves inside of us. One is Fear. It carries anxiety, worry, uncertainty, hesitancy, indecision and inaction. The other is Faith. It brings calm, conviction, confidence, enthusiasm, decisiveness, excitement and action." The grandson thought about it for a moment and then meekly asked his grandfather, "Which wolf wins?" The old Cherokee replied, *"The one you feed."*

Your journey to find your brave will be defined by the way you decide to use your unique strengths toward realizing the vision you have for your life. Your inner-strength will be measured by the faith and trust you have in yourself. Your faith and self-trust will help you access spiritual and creative powers within you to embrace fear as a gift while optimizing growth opportunities that help you manifest new possibilities in life.

One of the greatest challenges you will encounter on this adventure to *Find Your Brave* is acknowledging how you need to get out of you own way. Experiencing the emotional freedom you desire from fear, doubt, insecurity, worry, and anxiety is a byproduct of embodying your spiritual authority, believing in the truth of your enoughness and cultivating a loving and supportive relationship with yourself.

*No matter who you are, what you do, or what you have achieved. The quality of your relationship with yourself plays a pivotal role as to how your experiences impact your life. Developing a supportive relationship with yourself makes it easier to get out of your own way to grow forward and flourish.*

## Are You Your Friend Or Foe?

If I was able to eavesdrop on the conversations that took place in your mind today about yourself, would I have heard a supportive or critical voice? Are you your biggest advocate or your most formidable foe? Whether you are your biggest advocate, or your most formidable foe determines your level of self-trust.

Here's why. When you are your biggest advocate, you treat yourself with respect, love, and compassion. You stand up for yourself. You cultivate respectful, loving, and compassionate relationships. You establish healthy boundaries in your relationships. You maintain a healthy perspective about your value and worthiness.

Self-care practices of radical acceptance and self-love flows over into your relationships which makes it easier for people to be themselves around you, love themselves and you. You appreciate your talents. You develop and demonstrate an uncommon faith and trust in yourself which is built on spiritual practices that enable you to embody the truth of your enoughness. You believe in your ability to achieve your dreams and goals, even if you have no experience.

You feel at home in your body. You take care of keeping your body strong and healthy. You understand the feeling of aliveness, engagement, and motivation requires physical energy. Regardless of your age, you have come to accept and love your body regardless of how much you weigh.

You recognize that your body is the only vehicle by which you get to experience the pleasure of being human. Because you feel an aliveness in your soul toward life, you are extremely grateful for your health and body.

You accept your flaws. You are forgiving of yourself and others. You decide to make peace with your past to liberate yourself from dysfunctional patterns. This diminishes their influence on your self-worth, and what you believe to be possible in your life.

You take responsibility for encouraging yourself and maintaining the motivation necessary to pursue and achieve your dreams. You seek support from others on a regular basis to successfully achieve goals and manage difficulties. You perceive failure as feedback, not as an indication of your worthiness to experience the good life has to offer. The majority of conversations you have with yourself are loving, supportive, and respectful.

The voice of your inner-wisdom promotes the truth of your enoughness. It encourages you to believe the following about yourself:

"I am enough."

"I am smart enough."

"I am strong enough."

"I am pretty enough."

"I am talented enough."

"I am worthy of love."

"I am capable of taking care of myself."

"I am deserving of support from others."

Sounds familiar?

When you are your biggest advocate, you begin to align your way of BEing with your authentic self. You trust yourself. You live with courage and speak from the wisdom nestled in your heart. You trust your intuition. You care about your personal wealth just as much as you care about your physical looks and accolades. You are productive. You make things happen. Acceptance of the truth of your enoughness and your embodiment of it makes a huge difference in the lifestyle you live.

Iyanla Vanzant asserts, "When you know who you are, you remain open to new insights, new information. You also know that what you learn at any given moment will assist and guide you on the path to where you desire to be."

When you are your biggest advocate the *Find Your Brave* process outlined in this book will strengthen your connection to your authentic self and the truth of your enoughness. Through *The Brave Way* practices in each chapter, you will deepen your connection with your inner-wisdom, sharpen your intuition and discernment, and transform your relationship with fear by embracing it as a gift to unleash your greatness in bigger ways.

On the flip side, when you are your most formidable foe, you do not respect yourself or your truth on a consistent basis. You are critical of yourself. You show yourself little or no empathy. You are dismissive of your feelings and emotions. You demonstrate similar behavior in your relationships which makes it difficult to experience the intimacy you want to feel in relationships.

You are more attentive to pleasing others. Your needs and wants often go unmet in relationships. You are always doing more and making sacrifices in relationships. You tolerate people treating you in ways that were once considered intolerable. You're okay with accepting less from others while they expect more from you.

You are not at home in your body. You are constantly criticizing different aspects of your body. You make little effort toward strengthening your body and improving your health. You're never satisfied with your weight. You have been using your physical features as a reason why you aren't embracing life fully right now. Any sign of aging diminishes your self-worth. Self-love and self-care practices are on the back-burner. You push yourself to grind harder to attain a measure of "success" that's defined by people who are no smarter than you.

You have a tendency of spending a lot of time with people who have no concrete goals or aspirations. They have no motivation to explore new possibilities in life. Some of them have achieved success but, they're stuck in the glory of past successes. They have little interest in their personal and professional development.

Some of them may even use sarcastic remarks in conversations with you as an attempt to keep you in "your place". They speak about the positive change you want to experience as if it could never happen for you. You have a difficult time accepting yourself. So you wear social masks to be accepted by others. You avoid letting people see the 'real' you because of a fear of rejection and being alone. Believe me, we have all done this at some point.

You hold onto past grievances which creates bitterness and resentment in your heart. This state of heart clouds your judgement and prevents you from seeing that your thoughts, beliefs, words and actions are creating the quality of your relationships. These grievances prevent you from experiencing the transformational power of forgiveness. Forgiving yourself and others is necessary to transcend your past. As long as you blame others, you will not have access to the fullness of the power available to you in this moment to create the positive changes you want to experience in your life.

You will do everything in your power to avoid admitting "*I don't know*"! You act as if not knowing something is an indication of your character and smarts when it is only an indication of a need for additional information and understanding. You don't ask for help from others which results in needless suffering. You're burning yourself out as a perfectionist. You can't seem to accept that you don't have to be perfect to be worthy of love and belonging. You take failure personally which is why you rarely leave your comfort zone.

When you are your most formidable foe, you live in a state of dissonance. You are not in harmony with Spirit, your authentic self, and the truth of your enoughness. You are disconnected from the reservoir of wisdom dwelling in the seat of your soul. You find yourself contradicting the truth of what you know and feel because you're not grounded in the truth of who you are and what you stand for.

The voice of your inner-critic promotes the myth of 'not enough' by encouraging you to believe the following about yourself:

"I am not enough."

"I am not smart enough."

"I am not strong enough."

"I am not pretty enough."

"I am not talented enough."

"I am not worthy of being loved the way I desire to be."

"I am not capable of taking care of myself."

"I am not deserving of support from people."

Sounds familiar?

When you are your most formidable foe, your life is often defined by other people's beliefs and opinions about you. Your opinions are based on what "they" say. Your mindset is fixed and your heart is closed. You dismiss the truth that you have been divinely designed to rise to any situation and be victorious. In this state of mind and heart space, it's important that you are open to expanding your awareness and perspective about your spiritual authority, authentic self, and the truth of your enoughness, and fear.

Jack Kornfield asserts, "The retraining of our mind takes steady patient effort. When we are depressed, frighten or angry cascades of unwise thoughts tempt us with their stories: "I can't possibly get through this," "I will always be this way," "I'll never have a good relationship." These thoughts create a painfully limited and false sense of self. With practice we can feel the emotion that these thoughts produce, release and replace them with a wiser perspective."

Because the difference between feeling and emotions can be confusing to some people, it's important that I shed some light on this topic to expand your understanding of the difference between the two before we move on. Emotions are the *mental assessments* you attach to your experiences, whereas feelings are grounded in the physical sensations experienced in your body. Emotions are often in our head whereas feelings are inspired by our physical body and heart. Emotions create the stories in our mind about our experiences. Our emotions carry the energetic vibrations of our experiences. Feelings are recognized through actual physical sensations in our body which informs us of what is happening right now.

If you are your most formidable foe, the *Find Your Brave* process outlined in this book will help you disrupt the fear-based beliefs, emotions and behaviors you've attached to the stories you make up in your mind that reinforce 'lies of inadequacy' about who you are, who you can become and what you are worthy of experiencing at any stage of your life.

Awareness is the catalyst for positive change. As you read the descriptions of characteristics aligned with individuals who are their biggest advocate, and traits of individuals who are their most formidable foe, which group of characteristics resonated the most with you emotionally?

If you are your biggest advocate, you are more likely to believe that life is happening *for you* which fuels a belief that you can overcome obstacles and figure out whatever hand life deals you.

On the other hand, if you are your most formidable foe, you are more apt to believe life is happening *to you* which often cause you to feel like you are a victim of your circumstances. In this state of mind and heart space, you are less likely to believe that you have the power within you to overcome obstacles and figure out what you need to do to move forward in life. But you do.

## Self-Awareness

*In the space - between the relationship you have with yourself - and, the one you want to have with yourself - dwells the truth of what you want to feel and believe about yourself.* Sit with this liberating truth for five to ten minutes and allow it to penetrate your heart before reading further.

Here's my proof. You know what feels good to you. You know what is good for you. You know the good that is within you. You know the good that you can do and want to do. So, why is it you don't feel a sense of conviction about your ability to create what you most desire to experience in life? *My heart wisdom says that we fear being our most powerful and authentic self. Too often, we fail to recognize that every experience in our lives provide us with lessons we can learn that will be useful for our journey ahead. Your lesson in this moment, it is time for you make your distinct mark on the lives of others through your contributions of service. It's time for you to grow and expand, not hide and shrink.*

Imagine if you adopted the perspective and belief that your fears, doubts, and habits of hesitation are gifts to help you trust and believe in yourself. What if they represented new opportunities to expand your consciousness and uncover the brave you were born with? How would you and your life be different?

Self-awareness is the catalyst for personal change. Self-awareness expands your consciousness and ways of BEing. It is through the evolution of your consciousness that you start to own your authentic power, and make decisions about how you show up in life.

*Be. Here. Now.* This is a powerful mantra that will help you direct your attention to the present moment. Self-awareness and self-acceptance helps you to acknowledge where you are with a grateful heart while admitting the truth about the change you most desire to experience, and cultivating the spiritual, mental, emotional and physical strength to maintain the clarity, courage and confidence to bend reality and experience new possibilities.

When you're open to life as it is and you're willing to elevate your consciousness and accept the view that *life is happening for you*, you will pay attention and be receptive to intuitive hunches, revelations, and inner-guidance that empowers you with wisdom, often beyond your experience, to navigate next steps with clarity, courage, and confidence. You start to execute baby steps consistently with a belief that you have what it takes within you to achieve your aspirations.

Your baby steps will provide you with the experience that helps to cultivate a sense of *knowing* within you. The wisdom of inner knowing is that it encourages you to think before you act, especially, in an emotionally charged situation. It helps you to see and value your personal story, experiences, skills, knowledge and ideas. It helps to shine a light on your distinct strengths and how you can use them to serve others in creative ways, reach outcomes aligned with personal and professional goals, while you seek and create opportunities to be more of what you are great at.

Self-awareness and self-acceptance helps you tap into the intelligence of the mind-body-spirit connection. It awakens you to the strength of your human spirit. It encourages you to travel toward the freedom that dwells in your authenticity. Awareness invites you to sit with your fear and acknowledge it as a gift that points the way toward paths that will lead to experiencing more joy, aliveness, growth and expansion.

You are brave. Prepare yourself to take baby steps toward unleashing your spirit and soul from the shackles of conditioning that has kept your authentic self boxed in to the status quo. Harness the power of your spiritual authority to embody the truth of your enoughness. Shine your brilliance and succeed in ways that matter to you. This is your time to brave the way forward. Because bold is not only beautiful, it's badass.

## My WHY for Writing *Find Your Brave*

After publishing my previous book *Get Unstuck Now,* I began to facilitate master class programs to serve as a guide for helping individuals get unstuck, and get moving toward navigating new possibilities in their lives.

These master classes enabled me to get up close and personal with individuals from all walks of life. As you might have guessed, most of the participants identified their mindset as the primary reason they felt stuck. Through this multiple week program, many participants discovered the real culprit behind them feeling stuck was the emotional interpretations they'd attached to various experiences in their life. Many of them learned for the first time in their lives how the 'meaning' they'd attached to past and present circumstances had created the mindset that was causing them to be in their own way.

After each master class, I conducted periodic checks with various individuals to determine their effectiveness toward implementing the information shared during the training.

These follow up activities provided me with the opportunity to support their ongoing success. They helped to deepen my understanding of the challenges they were facing when it came to implementing what they'd learned during the program.

I discovered that several of them were struggling with a lack of self-trust in their ability to create and sustain the positive change they wanted to experience. *It's funny how life has a way of presenting us with experiences designed to teach us the exact lessons we need to learn for our growth and development.*

This dilemma troubled my heart. I was committed to helping students in the master class get clear, get unstuck, and get moving in their life. While at the same time, life was challenging me to get to the heart of my own truth. I had faith in my ability to teach the information in *Get Unstuck Now*. After all, it was based on my personal and professional experiences. However, I was struggling with the task of promoting and positioning myself and the ideas in the book in ways that would captivate the interest of larger audiences.

Despite the messages I received from readers of *Get Unstuck Now* about the impact the two-part book's message was having on their perspective of themselves and what they had started to believe was possible in their lives, I continued to hesitate to take the necessary actions to promote and market the book. This dilemma started to create an internal tug-of-war within me. I started to question if I had would it took to become a successful author. I started doubting myself. I stopped trusting in my ability to figure out the most effective actions to get on track. As much as I love, love, love to write, I started to fear that my dream of becoming a successful author was just wishful thinking on my part.

I was experiencing major resistance to 'go all in' toward my dream to be a successful author. The fear felt familiar to me. It reminded me of the time when I had to board my first airplane to travel for a business trip. The familiarity of the fear made it a necessity for me to get to the root of it. My first airplane trip increased my courage to pursue and achieve promotional opportunities within the Courtyard by Marriott which eventually led to my first general management position. This dilemma became a BIG deal to me. I could envision what was at stake.

I set aside time in my monthly schedule to brainstorm the issue from different perspectives. The fact that I was at the bottom of the learning curve when it came to achieving my author goals, I knew that massive action was required. Unfortunately, I lacked the self-trust necessary to navigate this path with the clarity, courage and confidence essential to putting myself out there as an author. I kept asking myself, "Who am I to think that I could become a successful author?" "Who am I to think I can help people get unstuck by changing the stories they tell themselves?" Over time, I began to paraphrase Marianne Williamson, "Who was I not to be?"

During each brainstorm session, I analyzed many of the actions I'd taken during my corporate career which helped me to develop a clear vision for my leadership. I looked at what worked and what didn't work. I reviewed actions that helped me to maintain an unwavering conviction toward the leadership success I aspired to accomplish.

During one of these brainstorming sessions, I recalled a conversation which had taken place a few years ago between a former boss and myself. I had just returned to my hometown of Columbia, SC and we met to catch up with one another.

As we talked, I shared with her how grateful I was for the belief she had had in me and the difference it made on the success I was able to achieve working for Marriott. She made this statement: "When I first met you, I could see that you already had what you needed to be successful. I provided you with opportunities to grow and simply got out of the way. You had IT before you met me." At the time, I didn't give much thought to her statement, "You had IT before you met me." That is, not until life presented me with a self-trust dilemma that had me dumbfounded. I could no longer ignore the agitation in my soul.

## The Power of *Knowing*

The IT factor my former boss was referring to was the self-assurance I had developed over the course of my life, primarily due to my success with bouncing back after major personal adversities, which I'd demonstrated during my initial interview with her, and how I consistently showed up as a leader while we worked together. *Self-assurance is not just believing in yourself, it is having an inner compass that nurtures trust in your judgement and decision making.*

Throughout my corporate career, alignment with my faith in God, and in myself, and the sense of *knowing* about my ability to overcome difficulty based on the "strong moments" in my life embolden me to believe in my ability to become a successful Marriott manager without a college degree and prior management experience. The expansion of my consciousness inspired me to trust my intuition and the strong sense of *knowing* I felt about my ability to figure things out.

I was able to accomplish this in the face of daunting odds. My 20-year award-winning corporate leadership career was a result of my faith, farmer's work ethic, and the willingness to work my way up through management ranks, starting from a minimum wage position to become an executive leader of several high-performance teams and successful million dollar businesses in the hospitality industry.

Throughout my corporate career, I was inner-directed. My leadership aspirations and most of the strategies I executed were deliberate and in alignment with what I believed to be the vision and purpose for my life and leadership. Early on, I did inform key decision makers about my leadership aspirations.

Never once did I ask anyone if they believed my lofty goals were doable by me. My history of being able to bounce back from several personal adversities at a young age had over time enabled me to develop an unwavering trust in my ability to figure things out. I believed in myself and my ability to make my leadership dreams a reality.

Although I didn't have a college degree, I never once believed the lack of one would hinder me from achieving my audacious goals. I became deliberate toward developing the business leadership skills essential to my success. Depending on a desired promotion, I enrolled in business classes at community colleges in the cities where I lived to get the information and develop the business skills needed to succeed in that position.

I took advantage of company sponsored training while raising my hand for stretch opportunities that exposed me to diverse decision makers and peers within the company. I trusted in the truth of my enoughness.

I had a track record of demonstrating courage, grit and determination to overcome numerous personal adversities, and achieve levels of success that seemed impossible. Based on these points of references from my lived experiences, I knew that my hesitation to do what was necessary to become a successful author had little to do with my circumstances.

**Cultivating Self-trust**

I knew in my heart that my dilemma had everything to do with what was going on within me, specifically, my lack of self-trust. Trust and faith are two sides of the same coin. Faith allows us to believe beyond what we can see. While trust inspires us to take action to create new realities. Faith is the vehicle by which trust engulfs our heart with a sense of *knowing* that we are often unable to explain to onlookers who question our thinking and actions toward a specific aim. We just know in our gut that what we feel to be the reality we desire is real to us. Trust is what allows us to believe that our efforts toward a specific outcome will bear fruit. Even when we misstep, we continue to trust that we are able to figure things out.

Trusting ourselves come down to a decision we have to make each day about who we are, what we stand for and where we are going. It involves moving beyond our comfort zone and believing that whatever happens along the journey we have what it takes to figure things out as we move toward achieving the outcome we seek to accomplish.

Self-trust helps us to become self-reliant which encourages us to not sit around waiting for someone to validate us or our choices before we take action to create the life experiences we desire in our heart. Self-trust inspires us to answer the call within our soul with no assurance that our efforts will produce the success that we seek. Self-trust fuels our audacity to believe in ourselves and in our ability to create positive change in our life.

Self-trust encourages us to honor the truth of what feels right to us. It supports us as we show up as our authentic self. It causes us to honor our word by walking our talk and fulfilling our promises. It requires us to disrupt the limiting assumptions we agree with about who we are, who we can become and what we can do. It enlivens our spirit and soul with enthusiasm as our faith empowers us to believe that all things are possible with God/Spirit.

## The Power of Self-knowledge

Lao Tzu once asserted: "He who knows much about others may be learned, but he who understands himself is more intelligent. He who controls others may be powerful, but he who has mastered himself is mightier still."

As I embarked on this personal adventure to revive my self-trust and sense of certainty about my ability to become a successful author and grow my training and consulting business, I took a look at my life from various perspectives which I was learning from the research conducted for this book.

One of these perspectives included the Human Givens Theory. This theory implies that each human has nine emotional needs. And, when we learn how to tap into our innate resources to meet our emotional needs, we begin to develop and embody emotional interdependence.

Abraham Maslow describes the highest function of human being in his studies as "self-actualized", stating that the highest quality they possessed was that they were "independent of the good opinions of others."

## Our Emotional Needs

According to the Human Givens Institute, the nine emotional needs we have as humans are:

**1. Security:** We need a safe place—an environment that enables us to lead our lives without experiencing undue fear which allows us to develop our potential.

**2. Volition:** In order to feel fulfilled, we need to feel like we have the power to exist autonomously and direct our own lives.

**3. Attention:**
We need to receive attention from others we care about and also give them attention in return.

**4. Emotional connection:**
To be emotionally fulfilled, we need to feel connected to other people. We need to experience friendship, love, and intimacy.

**5. Connection to the wider community:**
We are social creatures, and our brain is a social organ. We need to feel connected to something greater than ourselves.

**6. Privacy:**
Mental and emotional well-being require that we have time and space enough to reflect on and learn from our experiences.

**7. A sense of status:**
It's not enough to have a group. We need to have a sense of our value within the group dynamics we're part of.

**8. A sense of achievement:**
In order to maintain our self-esteem, we need to have a sense that we are accomplishing things of value.

**9. Meaning:** In the same vein of feeling that we're accomplishing things of value, we all need to have the sense that we're part of something greater than ourselves, having a coherent set of beliefs about life and what's it all for.

My definition of emotional interdependence sums it up as *a reflection of actions we initiate to affirm the best that is within us, we are inner directed, our sense of self-worth is defined by what we believe to be true about our enoughness, our self-worth is not dependent upon whether people agree with our enoughness or accept it to be true.*

*We recognize our need for love, for giving, and for receiving love from others. While we are free from our dependence on other people and circumstances to take action in our best interest. We respect and honor the interdependence of healthy, loving, and supportive relationships.*

This means that you and I are responsible for advocating for our best interests and meeting our emotional needs. When we do, there is no hesitation to share our vision, perspectives and goals with others for the purpose of advancing our intention to serve more people in a greater role.

When we choose not to meet our emotional needs, we exhibit traits of being our most formidable foe. We seek validation from friends, loved ones, and the public. We tend to isolate ourselves and focus on who isn't "being there" for us like we want them to be. We stop asking for help and support from others to achieve our goals.

Any efforts to advance our vision stalls as we pull over to the sidelines and become a spectator of life versus an active participator in creating the life of our dreams. Can you relate?

Emotional interdependence liberates our soul. It enables us to live with the freedom that comes from generating our life experiences from the inside-out. It helps us develop the emotional resilience necessary to stop allowing the opinions and criticism of people get in our way of creating a life that honors our authentic self. Our soul experiences a renewed sense of aliveness and joy as a result of aligning our efforts with the truth of our spiritual authority, authentic power and enoughness.

This is a game changer. Why? Because so many of us can recall during our formative years how we were conditioned to believe that our worthiness was defined by the external validation we received from others.

Many of us felt we had to "do" something to earn acceptance and love. We didn't always feel we were loved and accepted for BEing who we are. This attitude influenced what we believe about our worthiness.

As you practice and embody emotional interdependence, you'll become your biggest advocate. You'll take responsibility for growing and developing your talents. You will own the vision you have for your life, unapologetic. The *urgency of now* encourages you to stop waiting around for validation from others. You have the freedom to decide you are worthy of what you want and capable of taking the actions necessary to make it so.

## My Breakthrough Moment

This book would not be in your hands had I not been able to unravel an unconscious emotional pattern hindering me from standing in the truth of my enoughness to become a successful author.

Any author will tell you that speaking engagements serve as a valuable marketing channel for promoting and selling books and products based on their books.

Despite the fact that I would sell out most of the copies I had of my book *Get Unstuck Now during guest speaking gigs,* other than my master classes based on the book, I hesitated to initiate additional actions associated with promoting myself and the transforming message in the book.

I had a compelling WHY for sharing the message in *Get Unstuck Now.* Yet I wasn't demonstrating the determination that normally accompanies any of my work that has been inspired and influenced by a pivotal moment in my life, especially, when that moment required me to face a fear. My behavior had me wondering to myself, "What is going on with me?"

I knew from personal experience and research conducted for *Get Unstuck Now* that I needed to identify the thread of emotion fueling the story I was telling myself in my mind. It took me a few brainstorming sessions before I was finally able to uncover *the first time I had linked pain to standing out.*

The experience involved me singing a solo during my fifth grade music class presentation. Here's what I recall about that day.

When our musical presentation ended, my classmates, teacher and other adults from the audience shared positive remarks about my performance. Although my mother was in the audience, she said nothing to me about my performance. I did notice how gracious she was at accepting positive remarks from my teacher and other parents about my performance. After my mom spoke to my teacher, she left to go home.

I was accustom to my mother's emotional detachment, but, for some reason I had high expectations on this particular day that she would say something favorable to me about my performance. I had been in a few school plays before, but, I er had a leading role before. Because my mother rarely displayed public affection toward me or my siblings, I had hoped that when I got home from school she would say something positive about my performance. She didn't say a word to me about my performance.

On the outside, I accepted her behavior as mom just being mom. However, my emotional interpretation of her reaction meant I was showing off by bringing attention to myself, and somehow I was wrong to do so.

The awareness of how this experience affected me emotionally helped me to understand why despite my farmer's work ethic, dedication to personal excellence, and passion for my work in the hospitality industry, I truly never felt comfortable standing up to receive awards during my corporate career.

## What's In the Way Is the Way

During the process of identifying what was going on within me that was causing me to be in my own way, I discovered that my fear was an unction from my inner-guide to leverage what I'd learned from acknowledging and accepting the truth of the grief experienced after the death of my son Blease.

My fear of dying from a broken heart if I allowed myself to feel the depth of my grief caused me to suffer in silence for several years after the loss of my son. When I got sick and tired of being sick of tired of the anxiety and fear that had shackled my soul into a self-made prison, I humbled myself, and prayed to God, "Help me, help myself."

As it turned out, my fear was an unction to level up the way that I was showing up in life with the knowledge, experience, strengths, and talents I have in order to walk boldly toward realizing more of my great potential by serving people in a more creative and expansive manner.

My "problem" was actually challenging me to develop a greater level of faith and trust in God/Spirit and myself. It was asking me to acknowledge and make peace with the fear I was experiencing, so I could initiate the process that would open the eyes of my heart and enable me to see my fear with fresh eyes. Only then, would I be able to transcend my relationship with the fear.

When we are unwilling to acknowledge our fear, we waste enormous amounts of time attempting to ignore, resist or deny it. The eyes of our heart remain closed to that which prevents us from seeing our fear with a fresh perspective. All the while, our fear strengthens its hold in our lives. This causes us to experience unnecessary spiritual, mental, emotional and physical suffering.

Just as it was for me when I feared allowing myself to feel the grief in my soul from the loss of my son, my fear of standing out as an author required me to reconnect and ground myself in the *knowing* within my soul. By doing so, the courage in my heart would inspire me to face the truth of my fear, acknowledge it, and make peace with it.

During this adventure, I was able to gain the clarity to determine the steps I needed to take to level up my self-trust in order to pursue my journey to becoming a successful author with a sense of *knowing* that it is a goal I can achieve. My sense of *knowing* began to emerge as a result of spending time getting clear about what success would feel and look like for me as an author, and defining clear goals with deadlines to hold myself accountable as I navigate my way forward.

## Align with Your Authentic Self

Mark Nepo writes, "…learning to stay in our heart is not a distraction but how we prepare the ground for living a full life."

The fear-based messages in our society would have us to believe that when faced with fear or any other challenge in our lives, we should immediately retreat into our mind for the answers. It is my belief that our heart governs the course of our life. Outside of physical danger, I believe we should tune in to what's resonating from within us that is aligned with our authentic self.

Alignment with what is resonating with your authentic self is relevant. Think about the best moments in life. More than likely you felt expansive, optimistic about your life, in the zone, energized, confident, clear and unfazed by your circumstances or people's opinions about what you were doing to live your best life. During those moments, you took full responsibility for your life. You felt free to be who you are. You felt free to pursue goals that resonated with your definition of living your best life. You were generating your experiences from the inside-out. You were inner-directed.

On the other hand, when you feel "boxed in" by life or consumed by your fears, insecurities and doubts, you are more likely to blame others for the conditions of your life, feel limited, pessimistic, lethargic, tired a lot, confused, unsure of your direction in life and dependent upon people's approval of you and what you do in your life. You are less likely to be aligned with your authentic self. You are more apt to feel and believe that your circumstances determine what you are capable of experiencing in life. You are outer-directed.

Your authentic self is an expression of the wisdom in the seat of your soul. As you begin to empty yourself of beliefs and thought patterns that limit your ability to experience the best life possible for you, you'll rediscover the freedom that comes with being who you already are, brave, bold and a badass.

# You Need Desire to Experience Aliveness In Your Soul.

# Practice 1
# Dare to Desire

*Desire is a teacher.*
*When we immerse ourselves in it, without guilt, shame or clinging, it can show us something special about our own minds that allows us to embrace life fully.*
*~Mark Epstein*

In *The Desire Map*, Danielle LaPorte writes: "Desire is the foundation of our will to live. When you cease to desire, you cease to evolve."

Take out your journal or notebook to record your thoughts to the following questions. Write down what first comes to your mind.

Imagine if every fiber of your being believed you could have life exactly as you choose it be.

- *What would your life look like based on what you imagined?*
- *What would it feel like in your heart to live exactly as you choose to live?*
- *How much joy, peace, love and excitement would you feel in the depth of your soul?*
- *What would your ideal day look and feel like?*
- *What type of work would you be doing?*
- *How much money would you be earning on a yearly basis?*
- *How would you be contributing to make a positive difference in your family, community and world?*

Were you open to imagining new possibilities in your life? Or, did you dismiss the exercise as frivolous and continued to read? Why does it matter? The new reality you desire to experience requires that you access the power of your imagination. In the book *The Code of the Extraordinary Mind* Vishen Lakhiani writes, "Creative visualization is a practice of shifting beliefs by meditating and then visualizing your life as you want it to evolve. It's based on the idea that the subconscious mind cannot differentiate between a real and imagined experience."

Once you ponder on this truth, if you didn't answer the questions, go back and stretch your imagination by visualizing and writing down your answers to each of the questions. Lakhiani asserts, "Essentially this process trains the subconscious mind to develop a new belief…"

When you decide to unhook from any lie of inadequacy you've accepted about yourself and embrace the truth of your enoughness, you will bear witness to the following behavior. You will value your unique gifts, talents, spiritual power, intuition and creativity. You will seek opportunities to put them to use toward the achievement of meaningful goals.

You will begin to transform emotional habits fueled by a lie of inadequacy with self-compassion. You will savor your success for the purpose of internalizing the lessons learned during your journey. You will take actions that help you develop trust in yourself and in your judgement. You will accept your authority and hold yourself accountable for living your life on your terms.

**Hear Your Heart Again**

Abraham Hicks states, "Whenever you start guiding yourself by caring about how you feel, you start guiding yourself back into your Stream of Source Energy, and that's where your clarity is; that's where your joy is; that's where your flexibility is; that's where your balance is; that's where your good ideas come from. That's where all the good stuff is accessed from."

How do you want to feel about yourself? How do you want to feel about your life? Danielle LaPorte states, "Knowing how you actually want to feel is the most potent form of clarity that you can have. Generating those feelings is the most creative thing you can do with your life?"

Most of us are accustom to living in our head. When we dismiss any aspect of our being, whether it is spiritual, mental, emotional, or physical, we begin to feel disconnected from our authentic self and power. We are multidimensional human beings. Every aspect of our BEingness is essential to our sense of wholeness.

The truth is, no matter how much time you spend in your head, your feelings and emotions influence everything you do. In between an event (stimulus) and outcome is your response. Thought proceeds feelings (physiological sensations) which influence your emotions (mental assessments of our feelings) which then influence your responses.

No matter how much you attempt to deny, suppress or numb yourself from your feelings and emotions they are always influencing your behavior. Danielle LaPorte asserts, "Everything we do is driven by the desire to feel a certain way."

## The Energy of Desire

According to Rollin McCraty, PhD, "The heart generates the largest electromagnetic field in the body. The electrical field is about 60 times greater in amplitude than the brain waves. The magnetic component of the heart's field, which is around 100 times stronger than that produced by the brain…can be measured several feet away from the body."

Everything is energy. Your thoughts, feelings, emotions, and behaviors create your personal energy field. The emotion of love transmits the highest energetic vibration. The emotion of fear transmits the lowest energetic vibration. Your dominant energetic vibration creates a magnetic field around you that resonates with similar energy. It is possible to experience high energetic vibes in one area of our life while experiencing low energetic vibes in other areas of our life.

Many people trust the vibes of someone they meet for the first time, before the person has had a chance to speak a word. The awareness that your energetic vibes are experienced by the people that you interact with helps you to be mindful of the mood that you show up with in diverse situations. Your mood either drains you, or nourishes you. I am not an advocate for dismissing the truth of your feelings and emotions for the sake of putting on a happy face. I believe you should make time for sacred pauses which allows you to acknowledge your feelings and emotions in a healthy manner.

When we grant our feelings and emotions the breathing space necessary to process them in a healthy manner, this action is a demonstration of our respect for what we feel and what we think about our feelings. This is a healthy self-care practice.

## Honor Your Truth and Feelings

When my desire to have my mom acknowledge my solo performance went unfulfilled, I was disappointed and unhappy. Especially, after seeing her smile with other parents who shared positive remarks with her about my performance.

However, just because I interpreted her response the way I did, does not mean the emotional interpretation I attached to the experience is accurate. My mom is deceased, I will never know the absolute truth.

The fact that we feel a particular way because of the interpretation we've associated with an experience does not mean that our interpretation is a fact of what actually occurred. The meaning we attach to any experience is a reflection of our perception of what took place. It is important for us to be mindful of how our biases, opinions, beliefs, and emotions influence our perceptions of experiences.

Although our feelings may not reflect the fact of what occurred, we feel and respond to experiences as if they are a fact. This tendency is why we need to be mindful of how we communicate what has happened in our past or what is happening in the present moment. Our perceptions are influenced by the emotional state we are in at the time of an experience.

It is especially important to be conscientious of this fact in your relationships. Every person that you interact with view the world based on his or her perceptions which shapes their perspective about their life experiences.

Seeking to understand people's perception of any experience will always improve your communication and connection in relationships. Why? Because it helps you find common ground.

The truth is, so many of us were not provided guidance on how to manage the truth of our feelings and emotions. We were told such things as, *not to take things personally, don't let your heart control your head, don't get too attached, don't get your hopes up too high, and don't let anyone know they can get under your skin and stop being so sensitive. Or, told nothing at all, leaving it up to us to figure out how to handle our feelings and emotions.*

Many of us have been conditioned to disassociate from and deny our feelings because the adults we grew up around knew little about processing the truth of their feelings, much less teaching us how to process our feelings and emotions. For many of us, the process of reconnecting with our emotional self in a healthy manner is unfamiliar territory. Be encouraged. Your journey will be unique to the evolution of your soul.

There is no need to concern yourself about how fast this process will unfold. It is more important that you allow it to unfold naturally for you to integrate the insights, understandings and wisdom that you gain into you daily life. You will feel and be that much more powerful and happier.

**Healing My Soul Wound**

After coming across the Human Givens Institute framework of emotional needs, I decided to embark upon the process of healing the wound in my soul from my solo singing experience. I provided myself the emotional support I wanted but didn't receive from my mom on that day. Here's what I did.

I pulled out my fifth grade school picture and for several weeks, I hugged the picture of my fifth grade self on a daily basis. I imagined putting my arms around my fifth grade self, and telling her with a loving and compassionate tone how proud I am of how she stood up to perform her solo in front of all those people with no fear.

I reminded her of how being a part of that music class helped me to make new friends. I pointed out how the positive interactions she had with my white teacher and diverse classmates helped to diminish the anxiety I was experiencing about attending desegregated schools.

And, most importantly, today when I stand in front of audiences as a speaker and trainer, I do so with the same wide-eyed curiosity and level of self-assurance demonstrated that day during my solo singing performance. I thanked her for accepting the lead singing role in that musical presentation. Because it turns out communication is one of my signature strengths.

I took the initiative to heal my inner-child by providing myself the *attention, emotional connection, sense of achievement and meaning* I felt was important for me to feel the day of my solo singing performance. By taking an active role in meeting the emotional needs I had in that moment, I began to discard lies of inadequacy I had unconsciously attached to allowing myself and my gifts to be seen and validated by others in public settings.

Truth be told, there are still instances when I feel uncomfortable promoting the value I bring to others, nevertheless, I am able to ground myself with compassion, and an understanding of my emotional needs and how to meet them myself so that I am able to maintain the passionate determination necessary to serve those I believe I have been divinely created to help and support through my work.

If, while reading the description of the process that helped me to heal my soul wound and reclaim the truth of my enoughness resonates with you, here are a few suggestions: speak to a therapist, gather information about healing your inner-child or do something similar to what I did. I believe that if more adults would do the work of healing soul wounds that occurred during their childhood, they would live a much happier, loving, and fulfilling life.

When we have done all that we know to do to get unstuck and get moving, and nothing seems to work, it is my experience that getting physical by engaging in some form of physical exercise can help free blocked emotions. Because it gets you out of your head and into your body. Also, any effort on your part to follow the emotional thread of when you first experienced a specific emotion linked to a fear will also help open your heart and mind to your truth so that you can take the necessary actions to heal your soul wound in a healthy manner.

With both options, using the Human Givens Theory emotional needs framework can help you identify the emotional need that is not being met in a present experience or identify an unmet emotional need from a past experience to help you give yourself what you needed to experience to liberate yourself from this emotional block.

## Inner Resistance is Fear

In *The War of Art* Steven Pressfield asserts: "Resistance is experienced as fear; the degree of fear equates to the strength of Resistance. Therefore, the more fear we feel about a specific enterprise, the more certain we can be that the enterprise is important to us and to the growth of our soul. That's why we feel so much Resistance. If it meant nothing to us, there'd be no Resistance."

Know that when you feel Resistance, it is a surefire sign that life is giving you an opportunity, a gift to bring about healing, peace, and alignment with your truest and most powerful self. It is through this process that your awareness expands as your connection to the courage in your heart deepens.

## Make Feeling Good A Priority

You want what you want because of how you imagine it will make you feel. Take a moment to think about something you desire.

◆ What is the feeling you want to experience?

◆ Who do you have to BE to experience this feeling state?

◆ What actions can you take now to experience this feeling?

Everything is energy. Manifesting a desire requires you to radiate its matching vibrational frequency. Feeling good about yourself and your life helps you to create a vibrant energy that radiates from within you and attracts similar energy. This will increase your manifesting power. The Universal Principle of Renewal states: "Feeling good is feeling God and raising your emotional frequency is about resonating with the goodness of God."

<u>*High Frequency Emotions*</u>

*Love/Acceptance/Joy*
*Passion*
*Enthusiasm/Eagerness*
*Optimism/Positive Expectations*
*Belief and Faith*
*Hopefulness*
*Contentment*
*Compassion/Empathy*

<u>*Low Frequency Emotions*</u>
*Boredom*
*Pessimism*
*Frustration/Irritation*
*Impatience/Disappointment*
*Doubt/Worry/Blame*
*Discouragement*
*Anger/Revenge/Hatred*
*Jealousy/Guild/Unworthiness*
*Fear/Depression/Despair/Powerlessness*

## Open Wide to What You Want

The process of daring to open wide to what you want involves an acceptance of both the good and the inevitable struggles you will experience. Resisting this truth rarely works long-term. Eventually, whatever you resist, will persist. Instead of resisting the truth of "what is", honor it with gratitude. Here's why you should.

On the previous pages, you learned the importance of how feeling good about yourself and your life helps you radiate at the vibrational frequency of your desire. I want you to check out the high frequency and low frequency emotions list again. As you do, think about moments in your life when you resisted the truth of "what is". Were the dominant emotions you felt at the time high frequency emotions or low frequency emotions? Did I prove my point?

## Develop a Gratitude Practice

David Steomdal-Rast states, "Gratefulness is the key to a happy life that we hold in our hands, because if we are not grateful, then no matter what we have, we will not be happy."

Robert Emmons a key researcher in the area of gratitude has found that those that deliberately cultivate gratitude exercise more, sleep more, have more expectations for good things happening, had fewer physical pain symptoms, helped others more, and had more friends.

It can be difficult to surrender to the truth of what is while maintaining faith and trust in what can be. All of us are susceptible to being tossed back and forth by our feelings and emotions. This is a common human experience. Practicing gratitude on a daily basis helps us to re-direct our thoughts and emotions toward what we are grateful for even when we're experiencing a difficulty.

When I finally granted myself the permission to grieve the loss of my son, the practice of being grateful for the fourteen years he had lived encouraged me to learn about healthy grieving practices. I remembered how his kindness and compassion had touched so many lives. Gratitude helped me to shift my perspective on my loss. Practicing healthy grieving techniques enabled me to embrace the truth of my feelings and emotions about the loss of my son. The process eventually enabled me to heal the soul wound from the loss of my son while shedding light on a purpose for my pain.

To this day, I acknowledge my gratitude for having the opportunity to be the vehicle by which Spirit used to give birth to his living soul.

What are you grateful for in life? How do you demonstrate appreciation for the people, places, and things you have in your life? Do you express your gratitude toward people in ways that are meaningful to them? How have you expressed gratitude toward someone today?

It's one thing to think positive about people, it's another to make time to express your gratitude toward them. Build your gratitude muscle by developing a daily gratitude practice. Here are some suggestions:

- Start a gratitude journal. At the beginning of your day, write down three things you are grateful for. Right before bedtime, write down three things that happened during the day that you are grateful for.
- Mail a hand written note to someone letting them know how much you appreciate something specific they have done for you.
- Forgive yourself.
- Forgive someone.
- Enjoy life as an expression of your gratitude.

## My Healthy Living Chronicles

During the process of revising this book's manuscript, I finally faced the truth about my physical fitness. Although, I remain one of my mother's healthiest children, I have been slack about protecting the gift of my health. I am obese. Because of my height, few people would look at me and think that I am obese, but my BMI assessment says otherwise. One of my core feeling states is 'feeling strong inside-out.' My inner life was getting a lot of love and attention, but, my physical body, not so much. I decided to do two things, start a weekly walking routine and began the process of kicking my smoking habit by using Chantix. **Update: I had to stop taking Chantix.**

When I started my weekly walking routine, my goal was to lose thirty pounds within six months. After the first month, I challenged myself to walk longer and more hills. During the third month, I added a walk/jog routine three times each week. By raising my standard for living healthy, my goal of losing thirty pounds blossomed into a stronger desire to develop life changing habits that would enable me to live a healthier lifestyle.

My ultimate goal is to have my physical body reflect the strength of my inner-being. I have accepted this will be a process that may take more than six months to achieve. I'm okay with accepting this reality. Nevertheless, the mornings I lace up my Nike tennis shoes to complete one of several exercise routines, I do so with a smile and a larger vision of what I believe is possible by embracing exercise practices and healthy meals that increase my energy and help me experience a healthier lifestyle.

One of the benefits I've gained from a regular exercise routine is that I can *feel* my body becoming stronger. The stronger my body becomes the stronger and more assure I feel about my personal power. Each time I achieve a physical fitness milestone, the more I embody a stronger belief in my ability to bend reality in other areas of my life. Exercising in nature helps me to ground myself in my body and it makes me feel expansive. Up until this shift in my perspective toward my healthy living goals, I detested sweat. Now, when I'm exercising and sweat, I see it as a sign of my victory over the complacency I had had about my physical health and fitness. Positive change in one area of our life often influences our behavior in other aspects of our life.

There are four main brain chemicals that naturally effect your happiness and mood: (1) *dopamine* which motivates you to achieve goals and is activated by pleasure and reward, (2) *oxytocin* which is activated by physical touch, such as hugs, (3) *serotonin* which is activated by going outside and getting some sun, and, (4) *endorphins* which is activated by getting your heart rate up.

Daily exercise, positive emotions, meaningful engagement in your work, community service and hobbies, positive and nurturing relationships, having a sense of purpose and embracing fun while you pursue and achieve fulfilling goals will help you nurture high energy states that level up your manifesting power. Each time you set a milestone goal and achieve it, it provides you with a concrete fact of your ability to bend reality as your mind, body and spirit becomes stronger. The achievement of these milestone goals serve as psychological and emotional points of references of what you can do. This helps you to develop a sense of certainty about your ability to achieve your lifestyle goals. The achievement of goals is a major catalyst to eradicating complacency and leveling up your competency, skills, confidence, happiness and lifestyle.

## Self-Acceptance = Self-Support

In *Daring Greatly*, Brené Brown writes, "As children we found ways to protect ourselves from vulnerability, from being hurt, diminished and disappointed. We put on armor, we used our thoughts, emotions and behaviors as weapons; and we learned how to make ourselves scarce, even to disappear. Now as adults, we realize that to live with courage, purpose and connection – to be the person whom we long to be- we must again be vulnerable. We must take off the armor, put down the weapon, show up, and let ourselves be seen."

Granting yourself permission to embody the fullness of your authentic power, showing up and letting yourself be seen starts with self-acceptance and self-compassion. Acceptance of yourself - especially those parts of you that you find are "not good enough" or shameful will have a positive impact on every experience in your life.

Accepting yourself as you are does not mean that you won't maintain a passionate determination and the resilience necessary to become the person you aspire to be. It means you have decided to become your biggest advocate. It means turning your natural compassion inward as well as outward.

Self-acceptance enables you to pour from a full cup of compassion and self-love to avoid the resentment, frustration, and burn out that is common when you feel and know that your 'busyness' has created a sense of unbalance and stress in your life. When your innate emotional needs are met, you pour from a full cup which means you are less reactive and more resilient. You are capable of cultivating deeper, healthier, and more satisfying relationships with boundaries.

Your level of self-acceptance influences the relationship you have with yourself and others. Developing a healthy sense of self-acceptance toward yourself means you have an awareness of your strengths and weaknesses while acknowledging your flaws with compassion. Personal development is never about perfection. It's always about accepting, believing, and trusting in the wholeness of your being. Research has found that people who are the most creative, happy, and successful have a common trait: they are kind and forgiving towards themselves, regardless of their circumstances.

Opening wide to new possibilities in life require you to take baby steps toward laying down your emotional armor. As you relate to yourself with kindness and compassion, you will stop beating yourself up about mistakes and shortcomings. You will bounce back from setbacks stronger and wiser. You will become more curious and courageous in your pursuit toward experiencing new possibilities associated with living your best life.

## The Power of Your Agreements

In his book, *The Law of Agreements,* Tony Burroughs points out, *"Your agreement is your point of power*, and you can add to or weaken any idea or commonly held belief simply by making a choice. We have within us, in any given moment, the ability to discern, to decide whether something is working for us or not – and choose to agree with it and make it stronger, or to say, "Hey, I don't think this is working for my highest good."

You have the freedom to choose what is or isn't working for your greater good. You have the freedom to choose whether you are going to love yourself with radical acceptance and compassion, or see yourself through eyes of criticism, comparison, and judgement. You have the power to decide which thoughts and feeling will dominate your relationship with yourself. Refresh your outlook on what worthiness looks and feels like by reviewing the list of characteristics demonstrated by individuals who are their biggest advocate.

Who do you believe you can become? Why? Is your 'WHY' a burning desire or a mere interest? Do you want to become this person because it resonates with your personal values and how you want to show up in life? This decision is personal. It's not one that you should allow anyone else to make for you. It's a decision you should make based on discovering who you are, what you stand for and where you are going. Choose to believe you are worthy. Choose to believe you are enough. No one's permission is required, except yours.

## The Cavalry Ain't Coming

When I was living on government assistance in Section 8 housing with my two children and my son's father, it was clear that there was no cavalry coming to save us and change our lives. I got sick of settling for less in life. I couldn't just sit back and wait on anyone else to determine what my children and me was worthy of having in life. I had to accept the truth of my circumstances while at the same time decide on how I was going to go about creating the positive change I wanted us to experience.

After quitting my job and unable to find another one conducive to my children's school schedule, I was evicted from my apartment. I moved in with my sister Glendia. Having been on my own for several years, it was critical for me to do whatever it took for me to get me and my children back into a home of our own.

After reconnecting with my faith in God and spiritual authority, I knew I had the power to choose the direction I wanted our lives to go.

When I was offered the opportunity to work full-time at the Columbia Marriott as a housekeeper, I knew that I had to use this opportunity as best I could to attain my goal of getting us back into our own place.

With an unwavering belief and trust in God/Spirit, and, in my farmer's work ethic, friendliness, growth mindset and dedication to service excellence, I believed with all of my heart that somehow I would get an opportunity to use the supervisory skills I'd developed on my previous job. Although I was working full-time, I continued to apply for jobs at other companies that were aligned with my supervisory skills, especially since I did enjoy the work.

Four months after being hired at the Columbia Marriott Hotel, I was offered my first promotion with the company. I became the housekeeping administrative assistant. The increase in income helped me to secure a new apartment a few months later.

## Maintain a Compelling Vision of New Possibilities

Once I completed the training for my new position, I started to see how this promotion positioned me to interact with influencers and executives in the hotel. Because my mind and heart were open to the possibility of new possibilities, I eventually learned about the company's commitment toward promoting from within its ranks for management and leadership positions.

When my housekeeping manager Peter DeVries demonstrated his faith in me by promoting me despite his boss's objections, I was not only grateful, I was committed to helping him succeed. Because I was always asking him about his work, he started to invest his time to train me on some of his responsibilities which he eventually delegated to me. Within six months, I started to believe I could become a Marriott manager.

Despite my circumstances, I was able to maintain an audacity to hope in the goodness of God/Spirit and belief in myself that better was not only possible, it was doable by me. This or a similar mindset and heart space will be needed as you continue on your adventure to *Find Your Brave* and transform how you relate to your fear.

# Practice 2

# Embrace Your Authentic Self

*The authentic self
is the soul made visible.*

*~Sarah Ban Breathnach*

*When I dare to be powerful to use my strength in the service of my vision it becomes less and less important whether I am afraid.*
*~Audre Lorde*

An acorn dreamed of being a beautiful pine tree when he grew up. The acorn was given a book on positive thinking and he diligently read it, following all the advice on using positive thinking to achieve its dream. But as the acorn grew he felt himself changing into something very different from a pine tree. The acorn accumulated every book on visualization and change that he could find. He followed the exercises faithfully. The acorn spent hours visualizing himself as a pine tree. But despite all his efforts, the acorn grew into a massive oak tree.

Will you become the person you know in your soul you're capable of BEing? One of the most pervasive myths in our society is the perception that vulnerability is a weakness. Vulnerability is not embraced without some reservation, hesitation and fear. In *Daring Greatly* Brené Brown writes, "…our armor and our masks are as individualized and unique as the personal vulnerability, discomfort, and pain we're trying to minimize." As with most transformations, we have to have an open mind and open heart, and a willingness to see vulnerability different, in order to feel and think different about it to shift how we relate to it.

Our willingness to be vulnerable is the path to accessing the power of our authentic self. We need to be honest with ourselves about how our fear of social rejection and judgment holds us back from fully embodying the best of ourselves. The good news is that when we begin to nurture emotional interdependence which is a demonstration of self-love, our efforts strengthen our courage to be our authentic self.

We begin to slowly discard our social masks and emotional armor and allow ourselves to feel the fullness of life, like we use to as children. We feel more centered and grounded in our authentic truth. We feel more connected to ourselves and to others. Our view of ourselves, people and the world expands as we embrace vulnerability with a compelling vision of the person we know we want be in order to experience our best life.

Deep within the core of your being, you have heard the voice of your inner-guide encouraging you to be braver, be bolder and be badass in some aspect of your life. Stepping forward requires you to be vulnerable. When you have listened to your intuition and took action in the face of your fear, you discovered that what you had once feared was primarily the result of your overactive imagination.

If on the other hand, you decided to ignore your intuition and continued to live your life as if you didn't know there was a bigger truth calling you forth toward a new possibility, your fear-based thoughts and beliefs strengthened their influence on how you decided to show up, share your talents, and the level of success you achieved. No worries, we all experience this. I've been there, and expect that as long as I live, I will experience some measure of this inner-struggle. It's okay. We're human. Vulnerability is rarely embraced without reservation, hesitation or fear.

Vulnerability requires courage. Courage is the demonstration of taking action in the presence of fear. Vulnerability as a way of life challenges us to embrace the unknown. Vulnerability is a gift that helps us to grow. The more courageous we are about showing up in the power of our authentic self, grounded in the truth of our enoughness, the more experiences we have with being vulnerable. The more experiences we have with being vulnerable, the more familiar we become with stepping outside of our comfort zone to pursue and achieve bigger dreams and goals. The more frequent we demonstrate vulnerability, the more familiar it becomes - the less fear we associate with it.

Your authenticity is a gift of love. It keeps on giving as you deepen your love for yourself. Your soul is encoded with unique gifts, talents, and strengths that only you can express. The courage that you demonstrate toward realizing your potential increases your sense of personal freedom and self-love.

When you feel insecure in life, what actions can you initiate to nurture an inner sense of self-trust? If you lack a passionate determination to pursue a dream and goal, what simple steps can you take to reconnect to WHY your ambitions matter? When your aspirations are linked to a purpose bigger than yourself, your passion for life and creating new possibilities is energized.

Your perceptions of who you are, who you can become, and what you believe you can achieve and experience is a reflection of the lens by which you 'see' yourself and the possibilities available to you in life. Once you decide on how you will show up in life, it's important to identify the ways of BEing that will support the development of the character traits essential to living your authentic self out loud.

In *The 7 Habit of Highly Effective People* Stephen Covey shares the following paradigm-shifting experience which serves as an example of how our perceptions can hypnotize us into believing that *how we see a person or situation is the way it is.*

## The Man On the Subway

I remember a mini-paradigm shift I experienced one Sunday morning on a subway in New York. People were sitting quietly—some reading newspapers, some lost in thought, some resting with their eyes closed. It was a calm, peaceful scene.

Then suddenly, a man and his children entered the subway car. The children were so loud and rambunctious that instantly the whole climate changed. The man sat down next to me and closed his eyes, apparently oblivious to the situation. The children were yelling back and forth, throwing things, even grabbing people's papers. It was very disturbing. And yet, the man sitting next to me did nothing. It was difficult not to feel irritated.

I could not believe that he could be so insensitive as to let his children run wild like that and do nothing about it, taking no responsibility at all. It was easy to see that everyone else on the subway felt irritated, too. So finally, with what I felt was unusual patience and restraint, I turned to him and said, "Sir, your children are really disturbing a lot of people. I wonder if you could control them a little more."

The man lifted his gaze as if to come to a consciousness of the situation for the first time and said softly, "Oh, you're right. I guess I should do something about it. We just came from the hospital where their mother died about an hour ago. I don't know what to think, and I guess they don't know how to handle it either."

Can you imagine what I felt at that moment? My paradigm shifted. *Suddenly I saw things differently, and because I saw differently, I thought differently, I felt differently, I behaved differently.* My irritation vanished. I didn't have to worry about controlling my attitude or my behavior; my heart was filled with the man's pain. Feelings of sympathy and compassion flowed freely. "Your wife just died? Oh, I'm so sorry! Can you tell me about it? What can I do to help?" Everything changed in an instant.

## The Power of Paradigms

This story provides us with a glimpse of the power of paradigms: the lens by which we perceive, interpret and understand the world based on our unique experiences. Our paradigms can be hypnotic; they can put us in a trance that keeps us believing in our limiting assumptions about ourselves, other people and life as absolute truths. When most of the time our assumptions are relative truths.

Covey writes, "Each of us tends to think we see things as they are, that we are objective. But this is not the case. *We see the world, not as it is, but as we are—or, as we are conditioned to see it.* When we open our mouths to describe what we see, we in effect describe ourselves, our perceptions, our paradigms." When we develop the habit of seeking first to understand a situation or person, before jumping to conclusions and believing our assumptions without facts, we find our brave to connect with the mind and heart of those around us.

## Creating Paradigm Shifts

A paradigm shift is a mental and emotional break from an outdated or disempowering perception of yourself, a person or situation. Most often the outdated perception is based on conventional rules or emotional interpretations of an experience that hinder you from BEing your authentic self.

*Opening yourself wide to receive your desires will require* you *to see yourself and your situation differently, think differently, feel differently and behave differently.* Recall in Covey's story how he shared that his mini-perspective shifting experience came about after *seeing the man and the situation differently*, which led him to *think differently, feel differently* and *behave differently.*

Your perception of reality is a byproduct of your consciousness. It is only by dismantling labels of limitations, including your canned perceptions of fear that you will be able to level up the habits of mind, emotional and behavioral patterns that limit you. Loving your authenticity will help you to evolve into your most powerful and bravest self.

## Twelve Areas of Balance

In the following exercise, I want you to create a mini-paradigm shift in what you believe is possible by granting yourself the emotional permission to want what you want in key areas of your life, unapologetic.

The Wheel of Life is an exercise that helps us clarify what we truly want to experience in key areas of our life while helping us identify priorities associated with what we desire. It helps us close the gap between our current life and our desired life experiences while increasing balance between our different life domains. It provides us with a snapshot of 'now', what's working and what's not working, and what we desire in our future.

When used on a regular basis this Wheel of Life exercise can help us see how far we've come. Periodic checks (I suggest every 3 to 6 months) can highlight useful patterns and facilitate additional change.

I've come across many variations of The Wheel of Life. In my opinion, approaching the exercise from a holistic perspective like it is shared in *The Code of the Extraordinary Mind* by Vishen Lakhiani increases its effectiveness. Lakhiani writes, "An extraordinary life is balanced on all levels. Thinking holistically will help you make sure you don't end up winning in one area but losing in another." He calls his exercise the Twelve Areas of Balance.

For each category below, rate your life on a scale of 1 to 10, with 1 being "very weak" and 10 being "extraordinary." Don't think about each item for too long. Often the first impulse—your gut check—is the most accurate. Be honest with yourself.

In your journal or notebook write down how you rate each area of your life PLUS two actions you can take in those areas that you didn't rate as extraordinary to increase your sense of fulfillment and success. Use your scores and the actions you've identified that can help you improve each area as a reference while reading this book and during your quarterly and mid-year checks.

1. YOUR LOVE RELATIONSHIP. This is the measure of how happy you are in your current state of relationship—whether you're single and loving it, in a relationship, or desiring one.

2. YOUR FRIENDSHIPS. This is the measure of how strong a support network you have. Do you have at least five people who you know have your back and whom you love being around?

3. YOUR ADVENTURES. How much time do you get to travel, experience the world, and do things that open you to new experiences and excitement?

4. YOUR ENVIRONMENT. This is the quality of your home, your car, your work, and in general the spaces where you spend your time—even when traveling.

5. YOUR HEALTH AND FITNESS. How would you rate your health, given your age, and any physical conditions?

6. YOUR INTELLECTUAL LIFE. How much and how fast are you growing and learning? How many books do you read? How many seminars or courses do you take yearly? Education should not stop after you graduate from college.

7. YOUR SKILLS. How fast are you improving the skills you have that make you unique and help you build a successful career? Are you growing toward mastery or are you stagnating?

8. **YOUR SPIRITUAL LIFE.** How much time do you devote to spiritual, meditative, or contemplative practices that keep you feeling connected, balanced, and peaceful?

9. **YOUR CAREER.** Are you growing, climbing the ladder, and excelling? Or do you feel you're stuck in a rut? If you have a business, is it thriving or stagnating?

10. **YOUR CREATIVE LIFE.** Do you paint, write, play musical instruments, or engage in any other activity that helps you channel your creativity? Or are you more of a consumer than a creator?

11. **YOUR FAMILY LIFE.** Do you love coming home to your family after a hard day's work? If you're not married or a parent, define your family as your parents and siblings.

12. **YOUR COMMUNITY LIFE.** Are you giving, contributing, and playing a definite role in your community?

This assessment helps you to get real with yourself about key areas of your life. It is a way to help you keep the main thing the main thing in your life. In a world of distractions, this tool helps us to regularly check our commitment to ALL areas of our life. Based on your scoring, which area of your life needs the most attention now?

I suggest that you direct the strategies in this book toward the area of your life needing the most attention as your *Brave Life Project*. As you practice and apply what you're learning toward a specific challenge, problem or pain point, your efforts will deepen your understanding of the insights and strategies shared throughout this book. It will help you connect the dots and integrate what will work best for you right now. This process will increase your retention and implementation of the *Brave the Way* practices.

**Trust the Process**

In her book *Brave*, Margie Warrell writes, "…fear is a product of the thoughts we create, a projection of some future occurrence and often something that has yet to happen - something that may be unlikely to *ever* happen. Yet our imagination can amplify the odds exponentially and leave us paralyzed with fear."

Personal bravery is vulnerability in action. It's answering the call in your soul when life presents you with an experience of fear and requires you to face it with love and acceptance of your authentic self to level up your life in some way.

One of the primary intentions of this book is to create paradigm shifts in the way that you relate to yourself, your fears, your doubts, your insecurities, and your habit of hesitation. When you are consumed by limiting beliefs and thoughts, worry and anxiety, you suffer. As you embrace the process of relating to fear differently, this life-changing shift in your consciousness and behavior will turbo-boost your effectiveness and well-being.

On the surface, many of the insights, tips, exercises, and strategies I share in this book may seem simple or not difficult enough to make a real difference. I argue that simple, ease and flow are superpowers that are often underestimated in our hyper-competitive world. Do the work without judgement. Trust the process. Trust yourself.

# Practice 3
# You Are Enough

*Everything shifts when
you come into harmony with yourself.
~Panache Desai*

*I Will Know Love When I Realize… Love Is Not What I Say. Love Is Who I Am And What I Do.*
*~Iyanla Vanzant*

There are emotional payoffs to trusting yourself and not trusting yourself. You feel good about taking responsibility for your life. Or, you feel good about the attention you receive from majoring in pity parties and the blame game. In either case, trust is both and head and heart matter that requires a decision on your part. It's not somewhere out there, it's within your power of choice.

When you trust yourself, you take responsibility for your life. You are willing to baby step your way out of your comfort zone toward a dream or goal that matters to you. Trusting yourself is keeping the end result in mind as you navigate your way forward. You are able to maintain an understanding that everything you have to do to be responsible for your life is not going to be easy. But, your sense of trust helps you to maintain a steadiness within yourself that assure you that you have what it takes to handle what you will face along the way. You forge ahead with a beginner's mind, trust in your inner-wisdom, and a quiet courage that dwells in your heart. It inspires you with a sense of *knowing* in the depth of your soul that **you are enough.**

## The Tale of the Tape

When you lack trust in yourself, you won't take responsibility for your life. You live within boundaries created by yourself and other people based on lies of limitations. You will blame other people for adverse conditions in your life. You will major in pity parties and play the victim to get attention from others. You do not set goals for your life because you have accepted 'what is,' as if your life circumstances can never change and be different. You believe the lies of inadequacy fueling your belief, "I am not enough." You live a life that is well below your great potential.

I get it. When I was in my early twenties, living on government assistance in a Section 8 apartment with my two children, Dee and Blease, and my son's father, over time, I stopped trusting and believing in myself. I remained in a physical abusive relationship because I had disconnected from my faith in God and in myself, and the truth of my enoughness.

Instead of trusting in and focusing on the truth of my experiences which included: my ability to provide myself the emotional support necessary to move beyond my depression from my mother's death while my father battled terminal cancer. From working four to five days a week in my junior and senior years in high school and still qualifying on my SAT test and GPA to be accepted at USC-Columbia while pregnant with my daughter during my last semester in high school. To feeling lost after the death of my father because I no longer had a living parent in the world, yet, with the awareness and understanding I had at the time, I figured out how to navigate my grief, and the fear I was experiencing. I had many experiences that could serve as reasons why I should give up, and brush aside the hopes and dreams in my heart.

During this period in my life, the dream I had had of becoming a successful business leader was placed on the back burner in the face of my parenting responsibilities. At the time, making sure our monthly food stamps lasted until the next month was a top priority. I worried that these circumstances were going to define our future.

I was frustrated and disappointed in myself because of the choices I had made. I had no vision or plan for how to get my life back on track. I was certainly living below my great potential.

## How Are You Relating to Life?

In his book *The Clarity Cleanse* Habib Sadeghi, DO writes, When we're in pain, we tend to focus on the cause of that pain which can be any number of things - illness, divorce, loss of a loved one, a difficult relationship, feeling trapped in a dead end job, feeling depressed, finding ourselves all alone, and so many other challenges.

What we often overlook is that the issue itself is never as important as how we *relate* to it." The manner in which we relate to everything in life is directly associated with the meaning we've associated with the person or situation.

## Unlock Your Power Centers

Individuals that experience breakthroughs in life whether they are going through a difficulty, recovering from a difficulty or wanting to take their current success to the next level experienced a breakthrough in part because they believed it was possible, and they became committed to taking purposeful action towards the realization of a bigger vision they had for their life, career and/or business.

Oftentimes, the belief in a breakthrough comes at a pivotal point in a person's life when a habit of normalizing 'what is' has become emotionally unacceptable. The inner turmoil that comes from a heartfelt desire to experience better than what is being experienced becomes a trigger that motivates an individual to seek ways to alleviate their inner angst.

It is in this spiritual, emotional, and mental state you will become receptive to the idea that you don't know what you don't know, and you're willing to become a student to learn what is necessary to move forward.

You adopt a *beginner's mind* which diminishes your ego's influence on your actions, and elevates your higher self as the driving force behind your actions.

Inspired by your higher self to seek wisdom and understanding to champion your potential, any efforts to develop an awareness of the power within you, and how to go about activating it will support your efforts to engage the power of your authentic self in smart and strategic ways. The following actions will help you to unlock the innate power centers of your authentic self.

**Honor the Power You Already Have.** If you haven't learned how to, or you have disconnected from your ability to harness the power you already have on your behalf, you will live aspects of your life blaming people and circumstances for not experiencing the happiness and success you desire. Honoring the power you already have begins with activating your personal story power.

**How to Do It:** A simple way to activate your personal story power is to journal or write on a blank sheet of paper details about key pivotal moments in your life when you demonstrated clarity, courage and confidence towards manifesting new possibilities in your life while overcoming difficulties. Remembering these "strong moments" in your life will help you move forward with hope and a greater sense of trust in yourself, others and life.

**Connect with Your Deeper Sense of Knowing.** When you aren't clear about what you stand for and what's most important to you NOW you'll lack the congruence necessary to align and direct your spiritual, emotional, mental and physical powers toward a specific outcome. When you lack clarity about what you stand for, you will feel confused or worse incapable of creating the change you desire. When you are connected to a deeper sense of knowing within yourself you are more apt to have trust in your ability to do what is necessary to achieve what you desire.

**How to Do It.** You need to develop a habit of connecting to the wisdom of your inner-guide. In a quiet space, dim the lights and close your eyes, take some deep breaths, and relax. For the next fifteen to twenty minutes visualize your future self, three years from now. Visualize the home of your future self, and notice the following: What kind of place do you live in? What is the style of your home furnishings? What is your personal style? Based on what you notice in the home, what is most important to you in this stage of your life? What feelings do you experience in the presence of your future self? Chat with your wiser, older self and ask her or him questions such as, "What do I need to know to get from where I am to where you are?" and "What has been most important about the past three years?"

Ask your future self about a pressing problem. Once you bring the conversation with your future self to a close, imagine feeling a deep sense of knowing about who you are, and who you will become as a result of tapping into your inner-wisdom to receive guidance for your next steps in the present moment.

## Be Honest With Yourself

Denying your truth is a surefire way to undermine your self-trust. When someone is not truthful to you, I'm sure you have a difficult time trusting what they say, right? Although you may not think so, when you do not own your truth in a situation, and you make attempts to deny your part in a situation, or refuse to accept the reality of 'what is,' you're behaving like your most formidable foe.

This pattern of behavior makes it difficult for you to believe in yourself and trust that you will do what's in your best interest.

## Acknowledge the Truth of Your Feelings

Reclaiming the brave you were born with begins with a foundation of self-trust. Think about how a baby instinctively begins to roll over, sit up, and pull up on furniture, walk and talk. Yes, it is biology, but, it also the instinctive nature of the human spirit.

We were born with these instincts. When we were children, we navigated the world predominately by our senses. We were attune to the energy and power of our heart.

Over time, we were told to grow up, in most cases, that meant denying our heart and listening only to our head.

If you find that this is your truth, you may have to re-learn how to trust your feelings. Trusting yourself is being honest about what feels right to you. You need to know that you are doing the best you can based on what feels right to you and it doesn't harm anyone else. You have to trust your feelings when you have to tell someone NO. You have to trust your feelings when you know you need to rest. You have to trust your feelings when someone speaks to you in a disrespectful tone and you decide to speak up for yourself.

You have to trust your feelings when you sense an instinctive nudge to be careful about placing trust in someone. You have to trust your feelings when you know 'enough is enough.' You have to trust your feelings when you don't feel emotionally safe in the presence of someone.

Trusting your feelings is not about walking around with your feelings on your sleeve, interpreting everything that happens around you as if it's all about you, because it isn't. That's the interpretation you are choosing to associate with the experience. Just because other people deny the truth of their feelings and emotions doesn't mean that you have to, nor should you. Trusting your feelings helps you to be honest with yourself. And being honest with yourself builds trust in yourself and your judgment which increases your self-assurance.

## BE a Person of Excellence

If someone who didn't know you was asked to observe your actions during the previous seven days, would that person perceive your actions to represent someone committed to excellence or someone normalizing mediocrity?

Unless you do something beyond what you have already mastered you will never grow. In her book *Mindset* Carol Dweck Ph.D. explains, that individuals with a growth mindset approach life with a curiosity to learn. They believe their intelligence and talents are dynamic and adaptable.

Whereas, individuals with a fixed mindset approach life wanting to look smart. They believe their intelligence and talents are static. Adopting a growth mindset nurtures the belief that you can learn more, be more and do more in life. This perspective enlarges your capacity to become the person you need to BE to manifest your desired reality. Do you have a growth or fixed mindset?

Nothing speaks more about what you believe than the quality of the actions you exhibit on a daily basis toward the change you say you want to experience in your life. Being a person of excellence is not about striving for perfection. It is a commitment to show up on a consistent basis exhibiting your authentic self. It's stretching yourself beyond preconceived limits while increasing your knowledge and sharpening your skills and talents to execute important tasks with excellence.

I was thirteen when my mother died. Nine months later, I had had enough of being angry about her death. I didn't like how my anger was beginning to change how I saw myself to be. For most of my childhood, I had been a happy child. I refused to accept that being angry was going to be the way I experienced the rest of my life.

My diary had provided me with a safe space to express my anger, frustrations and fears about my mother's death and how my life had been disrupted. It was through the writings in my diary that I became aware of the voice of my inner-wisdom. As a result, I was inspired to trust my ability to move beyond my anger. I began to take actions that would help me feel less angry. I began to exercise daily and count my calories to lose the pounds I'd gained from the emotional eating habit I'd developed after my mom's death. I got involved with school activities which helped me make new friends. I got my first job at the Carolina Inn hotel as a bus girl. The combination of these activities helped me to lose the weight I'd gained, and process my anger and the meaning I'd attached to my mom's death. To sum it all up, by the grace of Spirit I experienced what author Marcus Buckingham refers to "a strong moment."

## Remember Your Strong Moments

One of the most powerful perspectives I have learned and continue to remind myself is this: when we remember to remember our strong moments and embody the wisdom we learned from these experiences, these moments prepare us to succeed when faced with our next challenge and opportunity.

Marcus Buckingham writes in *Find Your Strongest Life,* "The secret to living a strong life can be found in your emotional reaction to specific moments in life. Certain moments, in your life create in you strongly positive emotions – let's call them "strong moments." He goes on to say, "Strong moments are authentic and true – they conjure up within us strongly positive feelings."

## Cradle Your Strong Moments

When we fail to pay attention and cradle the "strong moments" in our life, Buckingham asserts, "We can easily allow our lives to be led by other people's wants. Buckingham encourages us to cradle our strong moments.

He says, "Cradling isn't merely holding. Cradling is a careful and creative action which involves the following actions:

◆ When you cradle something, you *concentrate* on it. It means looking at the moment from new angles and delighting in the details that you discover.

◆ When you cradle something, you *accept* it. You feel its weight and allow it to move you.

◆ When you cradle something, you *nurture* it. Your hand isn't closed like a fist. It is cupped protective of what it's holding but also open to the possibility of growth. When you cradle something, you are hopeful.

One of the most empowering strategies you can adopt is that of setting aside time on a daily and weekly basis to savor your success, and assess the insights gained from the lessons you are learning on your journey. This helps you to identify what works and what isn't working. Just as important, it keeps you emotionally connected to how your efforts are shaping the results and success that you accomplish. This is one of the secrets to maintaining the mindset and feeling of success.

## The Courage to Live with Integrity

The foundation of self-trust is built on your beliefs about yourself, and the integrity of your actions. It is easier to trust yourself when you know that you're living congruent with your core beliefs, core values, and what you say you will do. This doesn't mean you have to be perfect. It means playing the hand you've been dealt to the best of your ability. Trusting yourself and developing a personal standard of excellence involves:

1. Having clarity about your core values (what you stand for and what you won't stand for).
2. Taking pride in the person you are because of your personal integrity.
3. Keeping the big picture in mind which involves managing your daily agenda and priorities.
4. Establishing healthy boundaries in relationships.
5. Developing a results-oriented mindset to avoid wasting time on 'busy work' that won't bear fruit.
6. Having a clear and compelling WHY that inspires you to greatness.

7. Advancing toward your dreams and goals with the belief that you have the creative and spiritual power to bend reality.

Living with integrity toward our personal values and aspirations requires everyday courage. It is with courage that we are able to diminish the influence of thoughts of doubt and fear on the actions we take.

## Our Deepest Fear

There is a fear that many of us rarely give much attention to when it comes to embracing the truth of our enoughness. This fear is acknowledged by Marianne Williamson in her poem *Our Greatest Fear*. In it, she declares, "Our deepest fear is not that we are inadequate. Our deepest fear is that we are powerful beyond measure. It is our light not our darkness that frightens us."

Pull out your journal, notebook or blank sheets of paper and answer the following questions. As you continue to read this section of the chapter, keep your answers to these questions in mind.

◆ What would it take for you to believe *you are enough*?
◆ What would believing *you are enough* feel like to you?

- What would trusting *you are enough* feel like to you?
- What would showing up with a sense of certainty toward the achievement of goals that matter most to you look and feel like to you?

Was it difficult for you to answer these questions? Or, did you have a clear sense of what feeling like you're enough means to you? I'm asking these questions for the purpose of helping you to get clear about what "the truth of your enoughness" means to you. Instead of accepting my point of view on the topic, or anyone else, you need to have a clear understanding of what it means to you. Living your meaningful definition will ensure that show up in life feeling that you are enough.

You see, I've noticed that too many people in our culture accept a trending perspective such as, "I'm not enough" as the cause to why they are living below their potential without questioning if it is really true for them. I believe some of them do this because they are afraid of fully embodying their power. Why do I think this? I think this is true for some of us because we fear the alternative.

We fear our power and light. We fear the thought that we actually can create the life we desire if we would only commit to doing what it takes to make it so.

We fear the loss we imagine will happen if we truly embody the fullness of our light and power. The loss of relationships. The loss of living our lives as hidden figures. The loss of our comfort zone. Instead of challenging ourselves to live with a new standard of BEingness, many of us use the lie of inadequacy as a crutch. Who do you know that would admit they don't trust themselves enough to handle the consequences of embodying their power and light? Perhaps, you do know a few people that would. Would you?

So, instead of taking actions reflective of our power and light, we become information gatherers. We think and believe that if we can learn one more thing, it will help us reach the point when we truly believe we can manifest what we desire. I'm an advocate for personal development and action takers. And, I have compassion for those who are constantly in the pursuit of learning "one more thing" before initiating action toward a goal they keep saying they want to achieve. This hamster wheel can become a source of unnecessary suffering.

When we find ourselves in this activity loop, it means we have become effective at being busy - gathering information. Now, when this is our job, or we're seeking specific information, like you are now, by reading this book, AND we are an action taker, we are being effective. When this doesn't apply to us, let's be real - it's a crutch. *It helps us avoid answering the question: Do I really have what it takes to do what must be done to create what I most desire?* Our actions and inaction actually reflects our level of self-trust.

Trust is a head and heart matter. You must trust yourself enough to make baby steps toward what it is you want. It is the only way you'll ever know the answer to this question. Trust me. The longer you wait to make baby steps toward what it is you desire, the more your fear, doubts, and anxiety will strengthen the resistance within you. There is a cost to putting off what you know you should do. I know. Love and purposeful action is always an antidote to resistance.

## Reconnecting to Your Enoughness

When you view the story of your life from the perspective of your strong moments, you begin to develop a sense that everything that you've gone through has prepared you for this moment. When you're able to embody the energy of these powerful moments in your life, you embrace this truth about yourself: "I am enough!"

When you take the time to identify strong moments in your personal story, you become aware of your fascination story. You gain awareness of the unique strengths and talents that make you different. Sally Hogshead states, "Different is better than better."
You will recognize the difference your strong moments has had on your life when you make time to reflect on the following experiences in your life:

◆ **The Pit:** the moment when you realize during a challenge you were with no hope and feeling frustrated and overwhelmed.

◆ **The Journey**: represents the searching and learning that you did to find a solution to the challenge.

- **The Breakthrough**: where you experienced a paradigm shift in the way you saw the challenge, which shifted how you felt, and, the actions you begin to initiate.

- **Results:** the outcomes you've experienced from the consistency of initiating focused effort towards overcoming the challenge.

Now think about a recent challenge in your life. Answer the following questions in your journal or notebook.

- How did you initially feel about the challenge?
- What actions did you take to find a solution to the challenge?
- What occurred to create a shift in the way that you approached the challenge?
- What was the results from the action you took as a result of the shift that happen within you?

## Trust the Truth of Who You Are

After completing the *Clifton Strengths Finder* assessment, and Sally Hogshead's *Fascination Advantage Assessment*, the results from these assessments reminded me of the strengths and traits I normally demonstrate when my authentic self is fully engaged and effective.

The results from these assessments encouraged me to maintain faith and trust in my ability to become a successful author and entrepreneur. They reminded me to remember to remember my strong moments.

Trust the truth of how you showed up during your strong moments. Regardless of your present circumstances, you are a brave soul. You were born with unique talents and strengths that when mixed with faith, courage, self-trust, grit and determination will help you actualize your great potential.

Sure, you may have fears and doubts that cause you to hesitate to take actions toward your dreams and goals. Everyone experiences this. I challenge you to consider the words of Marianne Williamson's, *"Our deepest fear is not that we are inadequate. Our deepest fear is that we are powerful beyond measure."* Spend time meditating on what these words mean to you. If you knew with certainty that the power to create what you envision and desire is ALREADY within you, what would be your next bold move? Trust yourself. Baby step your way to greatness.

You have a choice: you can accept the lie that you are not enough, or you can choose to embody your spiritual authority and have the courage to engage the talents and wisdom of your authentic self and make your next bold moves. You have the capacity to rise and slay your greatness. YES, you can create a new model of reality for your life. YES, you can step into the driver seat of your life and start a new chapter in your life. YES, you can learn how to align who you are BEing with your highest aspirations. Embrace these liberating truths now.

*When faced with new opportunities and new challenges, remember who you are during your strongest of moments.* Leverage the hard-earned wisdom gained from these experiences. Use your wisdom to serve as a reminder of the truth of your enoughness. This truth never changes. We just disconnect from it. But, it is always dwelling within us. It awaits our permission to show us the strength of the authentic power dwelling in the seat of our soul. It only requires us to do one thing: surrender.

## Surrender and Allow

In the *Endless Practice* Mark Nepo writes, "Life is difficult and beautiful, soft and hard. It's fragmented and whole. Within a single day our cells are both dying and being born. Likewise, our consciousness and heartfulness is both fragmented and whole. Within each experience, our understanding of life is being torn apart so new perspectives and insights can rejoin. Like our cells, the very makeup of who we are is both dying and being born, through our moment-to-moment struggle with being human."

The slice of life depicted in this passage provides us with a glimpse of how much we control in life. So much of life is out of our control. I know how difficult for many of us to accept this truth. That is, until, we are faced with a heart-wrenching experience in which nothing we do - can change the reality because it's permanent. This state of surrender allows us to align with Spirit so that we can learn what we need to rise above a difficulty and evolve. It is through the evolution of our soul we begin to discover the precious gems that seek to emerge from within us because of our surrendered heart.

When you trust in, and surrender to the truth of your enoughness, you will discover loving truths about yourself. Such as, the loving truth is, you are doing the best you can based on your current level of awareness, knowledge and understanding. You will do differently as you increase your level of awareness, knowledge and understanding. The loving truth is, your point of power is always in the present moment. You can choose in this moment to change your thoughts, beliefs, words and actions that do not serve your greater good. You can develop new habits.

The loving truth is, you are an expression of the Divine. The loving truth is, you are powerful beyond measure. The loving truth is, you are brilliant, fabulous, and talented. The loving truth is, you are compassionate and kind. The loving truth is, your light is meant to shine so that others are able to see their way forward. The loving truth is, you are worthy. The loving truth is, you are deserving of all the goodness in life your heart is open to embrace, and then some.

# The Alignment

*I believe that the most important thing, beyond discipline and creativity is daring to dare.*
~*Maya Angelou*

A few years ago, on the dawn of my fiftieth birthday, I began to reflect on a long list of creative projects and health and wellness goals that I kept telling myself I would get around to doing tomorrow. Things such as...

◆ Tomorrow, I'll begin an exercise and health and wellness regimen that strengthens my brain, heart and muscles.

◆ Tomorrow, I'll start writing and publishing books.

◆ Tomorrow, I'll create a plan and execute it to increase my discretionary income to eliminate bad debt.

◆ Tomorrow, I'll get out and socialize more in Columbia and get reacquainted with new people and discover what's new on the social scene.

◆ Tomorrow, I'll start hosting regular empowerment and leadership training events for youth, women and organizations.

Do you have a similar list? Today, I am in hot pursuit of achieving all of the items on this list. Yet, I wonder how my life would have been different today had I stopped telling myself, 'Tomorrow, I'll…' I wonder about the difference I could have made in the lives of more people had I spent less time talking about what I wanted to do, and spent more time doing what I said I wanted to do. I wonder how my love for the written word could have been more developed and expressed in ways beyond what I imagine to be possible as an author. I wonder about the contributions my business would have been able to make in the lives of others had I committed to taking consistent action, even in the face of mis-steps toward growing my online business, years ago.

I'm not someone who spends a lot of time thinking about what could have happened in my life. For the purpose of this book, I revisited this list that sparked a fire in my belly to stop putting off for tomorrow what I could get started doing today. My friend, what are you putting off until a better time, a less challenging circumstance or you have more money? I'm not saying that your reasons are not legit. I just want you to think about whether or not you have been as resourceful as you could be.

We are the steward of our time and how we spend it. There's not one person that will read this book who wants to feel regret on his or her deathbed because of their answer to this question: *"Have I lived the best life possible I could considering my faith, knowledge, experience, relationships and creative abilities?"*

In the book *Die Empty*, Todd Henry acknowledges, "The most valuable land in the world is not Manhattan, or the oil fields of the Middle East, or the gold mines of South Africa. It's the graveyard. In the graveyard are buried all of the unwritten novels, never-launched businesses, unreconciled relationships, and all of the other things that people thought, 'I will get around to that tomorrow.' One day, however, their tomorrow ran out."

Now, my friend, the table is turned, the spotlight is on you. Will you be like the majority of people who live with the regret of what they could have done, but didn't do because they never disrupted their limiting assumptions or expanded the way they related to their fears? Or, will you start executing actions today that will enable you to create a legacy of your life that makes you feel proud? Will you major in reasons or results?

What message do you need to share with the world? What truth do you need to speak to power? What idea you can't stop thinking about? What leadership role you want to take on? What company do you dream of building? What relationship do you want to develop and nurture?

What group of people need you to show up to express your gifts in order for them to live a better life? Are you always learning and never implementing what you already know? Isn't it time to you stop dreaming and start doing?

Why is it easy for you to commit to the dreams of others instead of your own? Don't get me wrong. There is always a period of learning, mentoring, and apprenticeships that many highly successful people undergo as they pursue their audacious goals. Many of them use diverse coaches along their journey because of their need to develop different skills to scale their success. I do. Nevertheless, you can serve someone in a supportive role while keeping your finger on the pulse of what only you can contribute to the world with your unique ability. Always, always, be your own biggest advocate.

There's no doubt in my mind, you want to be more, do more, and experience more in life. You want to have a bigger impact with your life. You want to serve and contribute to the betterment of more people. You want adventure. There are more places and cultures you want to explore. There is more love, joy, passion and purpose you want to experience and express. You can begin to experience it all by disrupting how you relate to fear with a commitment to become an action taker. Be a doer.

When we have a hesitation habit, it is difficult to align our thoughts, emotions, and actions with the rhythm of our soul. When we do not live in concert with what we desire and value, it creates added stress and pressure in our life.

Everything in life is a vibration. Each individual soul has its own unique vibration. Our soul craves success that is aligned with its highest purpose. Living a life aligned with the rhythm of your soul includes, *mmovement that is in harmony with your deepest values and your highest self.* Any action that we take that compromises our deepest values and causes us to lose respect for ourselves diminishes the strength of our faith and self-trust.

Our soul is weakened by actions incongruent with our deepest values and highest aspirations. Our soul is strengthened by actions in harmony with our deepest values and our highest self. When we can look ourselves in the mirror and feel proud of who we are, and who we are becoming, and know with all sincerity the actions we exhibit toward people, our responsibilities, and goals reflect the highest intentions and our personal best, we are attuned to the highest frequency of our soul. In this state, we are much more conscious of the decisions we make and the actions we take to level up our happiness and success.

Pull out your journal or notebook. Improve your alignment with your values and priorities by getting clear about your answers to the following questions:

◆ What do I stand for?

◆ What contributions will I make with my life?

◆ What do I most want to experience?

◆ What do I need to learn to demonstrate personal excellence?

◆ What three actions can I take within 24 hours toward experiencing something I desire?

When you embody the mindset and behaviors that reflect your deepest values and highest self, you will live a lifestyle congruent with the rhythm of your soul. Your success will strengthen you from the inside out, and provide you with a sense of meaning and purpose that enlarges your faith, self-trust, clarity, courage, and confidence.

Brendon Burchard states, "Only action allows us to create grow, connect, contribute, rise to our highest selves, and soar into the bright stratosphere of greatness."

# Practice 4

# Show Up for Yourself

*Don't look for your dreams
to come true; look to become
true to your dreams.*

*~Michael Beckwith*

Despite the brutal realities of our world, we are tired of allowing the fear-based messages that inundate our society define what we believe to be possible in our lives. We want to face the truth of our realities with courage, not fear. We want to be brave. Because our authentic self craves freedom.

The word courage comes from the Latin word *cor,* meaning "heart," and so the essence of courage is about living "wholeheartedly." Therefore, so long as you have breath in your body, you have what it takes to show up for your dreams by going after them with the fullness of your heart.

Showing up for your dreams require you to nurture the courage in your heart to act brave. In her book *Playing Big*, Tara Mohr explores principles to help us move past self-doubt to create what we most desire in our career, our community, and our work.

In the chapter *"Hiding"*, she points out common ways brilliant women (and I add men) hide from playing bigger. Some of the ways we do so include, telling ourselves the story that "this has to happen before that", which is the notion that there is a defined path of actions that must be taken prior to us initiating bold moves towards creating a life and work we love. Other ways we hide from playing bigger includes, over-complicating and endless polishing (*when nothing never seems good enough to ship*), collecting or curating what everyone else has to say about it (*spending countless hours on the Internet absorbing information from other experts*), omitting our own story (*failing to recognize the value you bring to the table*) and getting more and more and more education (*just one more degree will assure me of the success I want*).

Let's be honest. At some point, most of us have used a combination of these hiding strategies to rationalize why we continue to play small when our soul is beckoning us to play bigger. No judgement, just awareness.

## Embracing Life with A Braveheart

Showing up for your dreams require you to make a decision to own your brilliance and become a shining example of what it looks like to live with a brave heart. My personal definition of brave heart is someone who feels compelled to take action in the face of their fear because *they decide* they want what they want, more than they are afraid of what they fear. How much more joy, love and success and abundance would you experience if you decided to embrace life with a brave heart?

Establishing clear intentions toward the manifestation of breakthroughs and the achievement of goals require bravery. Taking those first steps out of our comfort zone, which Mohr identifies as "leaps" requires bravery. Saying "NO" to requests and tasks that are not aligned with our intention to create a life and work we love requires bravery. Creating space for more of what we want to say "YES" to in our lives requires bravery. Standing up for ourselves requires bravery. Being humble requires bravery. Connecting with others with an open mind and open heart leaves us vulnerable which requires bravery. Creating a life that reflects the grandest version of our authentic self requires bravery.

Instead of holding on to the notion that only first responders and members of the military are capable of brave acts, let us choose to develop and nurture a brave heart. Let us become the heroes and heroines of our story. Let us rise up and become the grandest version of our bravest self.

## Take Strategic Leaps

One of the strategies we can implement to develop a brave heart is taking leap actions. According to Tara Mohr, *leaps* are identified as the following:

◆ It gets you playing bigger now, according to what playing bigger means to you.

◆ It can be finished within one or two weeks.

◆ It's simple: an action you could describe in a short phrase. For example, "host a workshop," "apply to three jobs in my desired field," "send a memo to my boss about my strategy ideas."

◆ It gets your adrenaline flowing because it stretches you out of your comfort zone.

◆ A leap puts you in contact with the audience you want to reach or influence.

◆ You leap with an intent to learn.

It's important to get clear about your definition of playing big so that you aren't dismissing your truth to go along with what everyone else is doing. Knowing what you stand for, and the legacy you want to create with your life will help you to maintain a concentrated focus on the "big picture" for your life. Keeping the main thing, the main thing is critical to aligning your actions with your values and the vision you have of your life. Your leap actions will empower you to occupy your "brave zone."

Remember, there is a reservoir of wisdom dwelling within you. Tapping into it requires that you embrace life and yourself with an open heart and open mind. While at the same time, you must be mindful to guard your heart. It determines more of your destiny than you have been led to believe. Make time to tune out the noise of the world so that you can hear the whispers of the wisdom within your soul. Pay attention to what lights you up. When you are engaged with activities that spark your passion and engage your strengths, they will stimulate positive emotions, create meaningful experiences and boost your capacity to achieve success aligned with the rhythm of your soul.

# Practice 5

# Disrupt Your Limits

*Don't dance around the perimeter*

*of the person you want to be.*

*Step in fully and completely.*

*~Gabby Bernstein*

Steve Jobs once stated, "Life can be much broader once you discover one single fact, and that is; everything around you that you call life was made up by people that were no smarter than you. You can change it, you can influence it, and you can build things other people can use. Once you learn that, you will never be the same again."

Consider the level of innovation and disruption occurring in all facets of our modern life compared to what was considered the "norm" just ten to twenty years ago. Some of which includes: the smart phone to Netflix, online book publishing to You Tube talk shows and Amazon's dominance of online shopping, to the rise of online education and training and Facebook & Instagram live streaming. Women are courageously advancing their leadership vision, voice, and value in corporations, marketplace and politics. Women are speaking up against workplace sexual harassment while leading social initiatives around the world. Disruption is a mainstay in the fabric of our modern lives.

Your life can be an expression of accomplishments that reflect your core values, top priorities, and highest aspirations. You have to be willing to disrupt yourself.

## Disrupt Yourself

Disrupters look for unmet needs they can match with their signature talents. Your signature talents are something you do better than most of your peers in your sphere of influence. When you are involved in activities that utilize your signature talents, it is easy for you to get into 'flow' and lose track of time. You are enthusiastic and passionate about these activities. Pairing your signature talents with an unmet need helps you build positive momentum and accelerate your success.

Most industries have pay-to-play skills that you must develop, implement, and achieve results with before gaining the credibility to scale your influence and impact. This fact is not a hindrance, it provides you with wisdom about what to expect when navigating new environments and new opportunities.

Take out your journal, notebook, or a few blank sheets of paper and answer the following questions from the book *Disrupt Yourself* by Whitney Johnson. These questions are designed to help us identify what we do well.

- What unique skills have you developed to survive?

- What makes you feel strong?

- What exasperates you about others?

- What made you different, even an oddball, as a child?

- What compliments do you shrug off?

- What are your hard-won skills?

Once you get clear about your signature talents, look around you to determine where you can match your talents with an unmet need. Look for problems and ask yourself, "Can I fix it?" Think about how your unique portfolio of skills would provide a solution to a pressing problem in your company, industry or community. When you decide to take on something new, be clear about the job you want to do and what will be expected of you in order to scale your success. Rule breakers position themselves where few people play.

## Disrupters Are Resilient

In their book, *The Power of Resilience* Robert Brooks, Ph.D and Sam Goldstein, Ph.D. write, "Resilient people interpret mistakes and respond to mistakes much differently than those who are not resilient.

Resilient people see mistakes as opportunities for learning and growth, while those who are not resilient attribute mistakes and failure to conditions in which they are powerless and have no control."

When you accept that mistakes are a part of life, and you do your best to improve a situation when you make one, you will remain in harmony with the rhythm of your soul. From this perspective, you are more apt to approach mistakes with an "I can handle this!" attitude. Brooks and Goldstein suggest, "Ask yourself what are different things you can do, either to change your behaviour so that mistakes are less likely to occur, or to change how you view and respond to mistakes when they do occur?"

It will be impossible for you to show up, shine, and succeed on your own terms if you are constantly worried about looking foolish in the eyes of others. *People have a right to their opinion. You have every right NOT to care about their opinion.* Those that are supporting your ongoing progress should be heard. And, if you are a leader, with or without a title, it is important to be open to diverse ideas and perspectives. Whether in your personal or professional life, just remember that whatever decisions you make, the buck stops with you. You are in the driver seat of your life. Be mindful of how much influence you allow others to have in your life. Get as much clarity as you can about a person's motive before accepting advice that suggests that you can't do something, or that something is impossible to achieve.

It's your life. It's your responsibility. Let's keep it real. Most people are more concerned about themselves. So, if you think that people are sitting around waiting to see what your next move will be, most people are not. Do you.

As you decide to learn from your mistakes, rather than feeling condemned by them, you are more apt to develop healthier coping strategies for dealing effectively with mistakes. You're going to make mistakes. If you can accept this fact and choose to learn from mistakes, you will approach life with greater passion and determination as you take action to redefine what's possible in your life.

Disrupters are able to maintain a depth of emotional connection to the lessons of wisdom they've gained from strong moments in their life. This supports their efforts to embrace their authentic self which illuminates their brilliance and badassary.

# Practice 6

# Transcend Your Fear

*May Your Choices Reflect Your Hopes, Not Your Fears.*

*~Nelson Mandela*

Fear thrives on the unknown. Its paralyzing affects are often rooted more in our imagination than reality. Think about a time when you were home alone. You're in the family room watching TV. It's quiet. You hear a noise coming from the kitchen. If you weren't able to identify it in a few milliseconds, your imagination starts to paint images in your mind of what it could be. Perhaps, some of the images seem to come straight from the last Lifetime television movie you watched. The next thing you know, your body is experiencing a flood of cortisol and adrenaline. Your brain has perceived that you are in danger so it has activated the systems in your body to be in fight or flight mode. You walk into the kitchen only to find nothing. You return to watching a new Lifetime movie.

There is a difference between fear and danger. Fear is an emotion induced by a perceived danger or threat. Whereas, danger is an actual threat to our physical survival. But, too often, we interpret them the same. Which is why our basic survival instincts are triggered and our body responds by dealing with fear and danger in a fight, flight or freeze mode. This is true even when our overactive imagination causes us to worry and be anxious over a perceived danger or threat.

## The Transformative Power of Fear

Life supports courageous action. Expect to feel uneasy about taking action that leads you into the unknown. This is normal for most people. You must accept that feeling uncomfortable is part of the price you'll need to pay to have what you have never had. Without full acceptance of this fact – you will allow your feelings and emotions define what is and what isn't possible in your life.

Anytime you change the meaning attached to an experience, your new outlook changes how you respond to it. Sometimes, the emotional meaning we attach to a past experience is not always on the surface of our consciousness. We have to go below the surface to get to its root.

In order for me to heal the emotional pattern keeping me stuck after the loss of my son. I had to get up close and personal with the story I was telling myself. It turns out, when my mother died nine months after my brother Arthur was murdered, my thirteen-year old self interpreted my mother's death to imply that a mother's heart cannot bear the death of a child. So, losing a child became my greatest fear.

Unfortunately, my fear of allowing myself to grieve the loss of my son caused me tremendous emotional suffering. In my mind the story that I was telling myself was, "My heart isn't strong enough to feel the truth of my grief." I was afraid if I had allowed myself to feel the truth of my emotions, my heart would stop, I would die, just like my mother had from a broken heart. My daughter Dee would grow up without her mother. My soul experienced unnecessary suffering for three years because of these distorted beliefs and unhealthy coping skills. I share this to place an emphasis on how our mind when flooded by fear creates an over active imagination that when left to our own understanding can cause us unnecessary heartache.

Our fears are often an attempt to wake us up from the spell of the story we've been telling ourselves. In many cases, our fears, doubts, insecurities, habits of hesitation or other challenges are gifts that present us with a path to expanding our consciousness. It is through awareness that we come face to face with the misperceptions we believe about ourselves, our experiences, other people, and the world.

## Turning Towards Fear

I didn't get my driver's license until I was 26 years old. Why? I was afraid of having a car accident. The story I was telling myself, "People drive crazy. Someone could easily drive smack into me and cause an accident." This story is a fact of life. Each time we get into a car, either as the driver or passenger, there is risk of a car accident. I told myself the same story about driving, until, *I wanted something greater than my fear of having a car accident.*

The catalyst: seven months after I transferred to the new Columbia Courtyard NW as a housekeeping supervisor, I was promoted into the department manager's position. I was determined to make the most of the opportunity. I said YES to the promotion without thinking twice about the fact I didn't have a car or a driver's license. I seized the opportunity and decided I would figure out the logistics of getting to work. I could no longer rely on public transit to get me to work because of the change in the hours I was scheduled to work.

There was a BIG upside to this dilemma. In my new position, I would be able to rent a home and move out of public housing. My children would have separate bedrooms, and experience a better quality of life. If I couldn't get back and forth to work, I wouldn't be able to afford moving my children out of public housing. There was no doubt in my mind what I was going to do.

Despite my fear of having a car accident, I made up my mind that I was not going to allow my fear of driving get in the way of making my children's life better. This wasn't something I was merely thinking about doing. In my mind, I told myself, *"I must do this."* According to Brendon Burchard, "When we have a sense of necessity to take an action is usually involves our sense of identity, our obsessions, duty or deadlines."

My thoughts and actions were directed toward two outcomes: get my driver's license and purchase a car. Instead of dwelling on the fact that I could have a car accident, my faith, thoughts and energy were directed toward taking actions that were going to support my efforts of creating a new reality for my family. Tony Robbins says,

"Controlled focus is like a laser beam that can cut through anything that seems to be stopping you."

With the help of my brother Laronzo, I received my driver's permit, purchased my first car, a Plymouth Horizon, and then got my license. Yes, I had my car before passing my driving test for my license. This experience became a strong moment I would refer to often in the face of different fears I would have to embrace as the trajectory of my career shifted upward.

## Heights and Flying, Oh My!

I was afraid of flying on a plane. So why didn't my fear stop me in 1990 from boarding an American Airlines plane in my hometown of Columbia, SC to travel to Raleigh, NC? How was I able to wave good-bye to my two small children and my husband, at the time, as I prepared to board a plane that would ascend to heights I had never been before? *I had a compelling "WHY".*

If I had allowed my fear of heights and flying dictate my actions, I would not have had the pleasure of being a member of the Courtyard by Marriott Mid-Atlantic opening hotel task team. I would not have been able to seize this stretch opportunity to expose myself to peers and executive decision makers from across our region and corporate office. Shortly after this assignment, I was promoted into my next management position and chosen to become a charter member of the Courtyard by Marriott Mid-Atlantic Diversity Council.

The exposure received from taking advantage of this opportunity was a tremendous boost to my faith which increased my sense of certainty toward making the progress necessary to achieve what was an audacious goal for me at the time: become a Marriott General Manager. I worked at the Columbia Courtyard by Marriott NW location (now Baymont Inn Hotel & Suites) for six and half years. During that time, I received five management promotions.

**Navigating the Unknown**

I became the GM at Marriott's Fairfield Inn in Wilmington, NC on February 9, 1995. Six months later, my teenage son Blease died unexpected from cardiac arrest. After his homegoing service, my daughter Dee and I returned to Wilmington. I took two weeks off to get a grip on my thoughts and emotions in the face of the harshness of my new reality. I wasn't sure if I could handle the responsibility of managing this million-dollar business with the emotional stress that both my daughter and I were experiencing. For the first time in my career, I began to question if I made the right move considering the fact that all my family and close friends were back in my hometown.

Three months later, I received the results from the hotel's employee opinion survey. The majority of the hotel staff had rated me the least effective general manager in our region. My mind became consumed with anxious thoughts. I wasn't afraid of losing my job. I was more concerned about whether or not I should request a transfer back to my hometown to be around those who knew me and would support my daughter and I through our grieving process.

I didn't speak about the results with anyone. Later on that evening when I got home, I began to give much thought to transferring back to Columbia, SC. I couldn't fathom how I was going to deal with this reality of the hotel's staff perception of me as a leader while trying to navigate the loss of my son. The results from the employee opinion survey felt like another sucker punch. For the first time during my career with the company, I felt as if I was working with a team that didn't believe in my leadership.

Whispers in my soul encouraged me to think about all the sacrifices and work it had taken for me to achieve my GM's position. My farmer's work ethic was evident in the results, raises and awards I received during the time I worked in Marriott's full-service and Courtyard divisions. And, I still had my daughter Dee to take care of. I was angry. I was sad. And, I was refusing to give myself permission to grieve the loss of my son.

I didn't speak to the staff about the results for weeks. I leaned into my inner-wisdom for guidance. One day while walking the hotel property, I had this thought, "I must figure out how to *relate* to this team to bring out the best in them." In this moment, I was reminded of my desire to be a great leader and what that meant to me. It meant I was required to learn how to serve the very people that perceived me to be an ineffective leader. It meant that I had to be true to the way that I saw myself, regardless of their current opinion of me as a general manager. It meant that I wasn't about to allow the sacrifices I'd made throughout my career go up in smoke without deliberate action to become the GM I had always believed I could be.

Serving all meant disrupting the outdated perceptions I'd held about how a general manager shows up and what a general manager should do to be effective and highly successful. I knew how to build successful teams. I made up in my mind that I would figure out a way to build a successful team with individuals who initially did not believe and trust in my leadership. At the time, I knew accomplishing this would become one of my greatest professional comebacks.

I borrowed a strategy from my management tool kit and scheduled one-on-one conversations with each team member. This was the only time I spoke to the staff about the results from the survey. During our conversations, I realized that many of their perceptions about me were things did control. After receiving feedback from them about what I should STOP, START & CONTINUE to be the leader they needed me to be, I was able to gain a better understanding of how I needed to show up for them.

During the conversations, we discussed their aspirations and what they were willing to commit to toward helping our hotel succeed. Because of their honest feedback during these one-on-one sessions, I discovered ways to best lead this team forward to achieve the success I believed we were capable of accomplishing together.

Within 18 months, I was recognized by the company for improvements in my employee opinion survey. During my third year as GM, our team won four #1 awards related to key performance indicators out of over 300 hotels in the U.S. None of these achievements would have been a part of my body of work had I allowed my fear of the unknown and my grief convince me I needed to return to the comfort zone of my hometown.

Yes, I was embarrassed by my first employee survey as a general manager. But, because of the results, I disrupted my perceptions of what a successful general manager acts like and began to embrace a leadership style that focused my time, energy and effort toward sharing power while building a staff of leaders without titles. Together, we achieved a multitude of successes that many deemed impossible.

## Transcending Fear

You can learn how to embrace fear with courageous confidence and become a fear-tamer.

**Becoming a fear-tamer consists of:**
1. Acknowledging your fear.
2. Deciding you want what you want, more than you fear your fear.
3. Disrupting your disempowering perceptions about fear.
4. Identifying a compelling WHY you 'must' take action, now.

I am using the word fear-tamer intentionally. Because, as long as we live, most of us will have the sensory ability to feel frighten, scared, worried, anxious, apprehensive etc. We will feel fear. But, that doesn't mean we cannot learn how to manage our relationship with fear so that it no longer boxes our life into a small replica of what it could be.

Fear tamers do not subscribe to the notion of denying and suppressing their feelings and emotions. They know from experience that what's in the way points the way to the freedom their soul craves. They prefer to process their thoughts, feelings and emotions in a healthy manner to maintain an open heart, and experience more joy, love, passion, creativity and success.

**Pain and Pleasure**

Too often, our feelings and emotions do not get the respect they deserve. When we experience a difficult feeling or emotion, many of us attempt to deny, suppress and disassociate from it. We do this to protect ourselves. Primarily, because we don't believe we can handle the truth of our emotions.

The first strategy you need to apply toward taming fear is an insight I mentioned in the chapter *Dare to Desire*. ***The insight: everything you do is motivated by how you want to feel.*** Why do you want to lose weight? To feel attractive, strong and healthy. Why do you want to be in a relationship? To feel loved and connected to someone special.

Why do you want to build a successful career/business? To feel you are accomplished and in control of your destiny. Every aspiration you have is a means to achieving a desired feeling state.

Think about a goal that is important to you. How do you want to feel as a result of achieving it? This feeling fuels your motivation towards the achievement of it. This feeling is connected to one or many of your innate emotional needs.

So, ask yourself, what do you want to feel instead of fear in your situation? What will be the pleasure you will gain from this emotion versus fear? How will this desired feeling and emotion inspire you to take positive action toward a new possibility in your life? You have to get yourself to the point where you want what you want more than you fear what you fear can happen. Recall my fear of driving story.

The second strategy that's crucial to helping you tame fear is: *what you link pain to and what you link pleasure to influences which actions you are willing or not willing to take towards the positive change you desire.* According to Tony Robbins, this is the most important lesson to learn in life.

Think about this: whatever emotional association (meaning) you link to any experience influences your perception, and the actions you initiate toward it. Consider something you've always told yourself you were too afraid to do. What is the pain you've associated with doing it? Is it possible that other people take pleasure in doing it? In most cases, the answer is yes.

There are people who are willing to do things you fear because they've associated pleasure with the act itself. Whereas, there are people who aren't willing to do things that you do because they've associated pain with the action. Are you grasping how whatever actions you have linked to pleasure and pain are shaping your destiny?

Although I wasn't conscious of this earlier in my life, each time I faced a fear head on, I was creating neuro-associations that linked facing fear to growth, expansion, and pleasure. This was in part due to linking learning in kindergarten with pleasure. Most of the fears experienced in my life have been gifts that when faced head on presented me with opportunities to learn, grow and expand in some aspect of my life.

When I began the adventure of reclaiming the truth of my enoughness, I realized the process of healing the emotional wound from my fifth grade solo performance has become pivotal to accessing innate resources within me that are helping to develop a sense of certainty about becoming a successful author and entrepreneur.

Today, I'm so grateful that my soul would not allow me to dismiss the dilemma of lacking the self-assurance necessary for me to show up, shine, and succeed in this next stage of my career. I remind myself of the pleasure, joy, and enthusiasm I experience from helping people find their wings and soar. Just typing those words flooded my body with feel good hormones. I am re-energizing my authentic power. It feels good to be grounded in the knowing that I have it within me to level up my ability to feel and experience more joy, happiness, abundance and success.

## Tune In to Your Intuition

Albert Einstein once said: "The intuitive mind is a sacred gift and the rational mind is a faithful servant. We have created a society that honors the servant and has forgotten the gift."

Intuition literally means learning from within. When you tune in to your intuition, you are connecting your logical brain and creative brain to the divine energy that is within you. Intuition is a heightened level of consciousness inspired by your physical senses, state of receptivity, and insights and wisdom from your higher self. When you try to figure out everything 'in your head,' decision making and progress can often stall. When you spend so much time in your head, it is easy to become crippled by the fear of making a wrong decision.

This fear when left unchecked can cause you to compromise your dreams and desires for the sake of pleasing others, and living up to some 'acceptable' social norm that stifles your passion and enthusiasm toward living the life of your dreams.

On the other hand, when you set aside time for sacred pauses that help you immerse your soul into the universal energy of life which connects you to all knowledge, you will begin to receive direct signals from your higher self for navigating your way forward.

The more attune you are to your intuition, the more you'll be able to read people and situations quickly and accurately, and, the more you'll find yourself instinctively "making the right choice."

Like most of us, you were probably not taught how to use your intuitive sense. Nevertheless, we all recognize it through our gut feelings. Trusting in our intuition results in it becoming stronger.

The following exercise will help you work directly with your intuition to strengthen your connection to the wisdom already within you.

Stop for a moment and IMAGINE the positive impact on your relationships, career, finances, and happiness when you consistently make decisions based on a sense of *knowing* that has been cultivated by your authentic self and intuitive messages from your inner guide.

- Find a quiet place to sit comfortably.
- Slowly inhale your breath on a count of 8. Hold your breath for a count of 8. Slowly exhale your breath for a count of 8. Do this 3 times. Each time you do, allow yourself to become more and more relaxed.
- Once you're relaxed, identify an event or situation that you'd like more insight about.
- Focus on the event or situation intently for a few minutes.
- Ask Spirit for a direct intuitive experience about it.
- Let it go.

Take the path of least resistance by detaching from the outcome and practice patience. Stay alert for signs of synchronicity that will provide you with additional information. Plant seeds of what you desire by providing assistance and support to others as you are able. Remain in a state of gratitude and appreciation for your life. Choose joy. Trust in that which shows up and resonates with your soul's desire.

# The Ascension

Your soul craves the freedom to express its authentic self. Throughout this book, life is presenting you with many gifts. The gift of embracing the truth of your enoughness by using evidence from your personal life story to debunk any "I am not enough" narrative you have believed about yourself. The gift of developing the self-assurance necessary to have a sense of *knowing* about your ability to achieve audacious goals. The gift of disrupting your perceptions about fear so that your soul is liberated from disempowering patterns that do not serve your greater good.

The gift of tapping into a greater measure of your innate resources to meet your emotional needs. The gift of creating experiences that reflect your desired feeling states. The gift of developing a resolve towards who you are becoming and what you stand for. When you accept, embrace and embody these gifts with an open mind and open heart, you will discover treasures within yourself that will become some of your most prized possessions. They will illuminate the brilliance, bravery, and badassary within you.

Becoming a disrupter and fear tamer helps you to establish an identity that will distinguish you because of your willingness to stand up for what matters to you, and speak your truth, instead of fitting in with the status quo, you show up in the power of your authentic self, instead of constantly comparing yourself to others, you embrace your imperfections and gifts with gratitude, you choose to be a creator instead of always a consumer, and, you decide to take leaps toward achieving the success you desire instead of living life on the sidelines and never realizing your great potential.

Your ability to direct your strengths, talents, and creativity toward activities that inspire the expression of your greatness enables you to live with a clear sense of direction that nurtures a brave heart. This state of consciousness enables you to ground yourself with a clear vision of the difference you can make in the lives of others. This compelling vision inspires a sense of certainty toward the realization of your vision because you trust yourself to make it happen.

## What Will Your Verse Be?

Living a life that makes a positive difference in the life of others has been important to me ever since I listened to snippets of Martin Luther King Jr.'s speech *I Have A Dream* on the radio after his assassination. His words inspired me to believe that one day I would become a leader that made a difference in the lives of others. From that point forward this belief helped to shape my personal identity.

This belief helped me to develop my capacity to anticipate and serve the needs of my internal and external customers while working as a bus girl, waitress, cafeteria line server, storeroom supervisor, housekeeper to my management and executive leadership roles leading high performance teams and managing successful million-dollar businesses. Two of my all-time favorite verses from a poem is by Walt Whitman which states: "That you are here-that life exists and identity. That the powerful play goes on, and you may contribute a verse." Source: Leaves of Grass (1892)

What verse will your ideas, knowledge, experience, and skills contribute to the betterment of yourself and others? It is your responsibility to share them. This is true, even if you are shy and reluctant to share your voice and vision. You are the guardian of your talents.

**Live Your Legacy Now**

Tom Rath says, "You cannot be anything you want to be – but you can be a lot more of who you already are." This is an important truth. Too many people fail to get to know themselves, so they waste a lot of time, energy, and resources attempting to be like someone else only to find out they aren't gifted for the demands required of a particular position or role.

The various questions in this book have served to help you develop an awareness of your unique talents and how they add value. This value will be recognized by others as you apply the practices and integrate the insights you are gaining from this book into your daily life.

Because your unique talents are natural to you, you may not think they're a big deal. But, they are. And people notice them even if they don't say anything to you. So, stop dismissing the complements you receive from people because, they are often recognizing your unique talents.

When your unique talents are aligned with tasks, activities and people who strengthen you, you will experience more "in the zone" experiences, enjoy what you're doing and who you are doing it with. Whether it's building a successful family, community, career or business, when you are operating in the "genius zone" you feel a sense of aliveness in your soul, you feel what you do matters, and you feel more satisfied, and, you feel a greater sense of purpose from the actions you take. Build a legacy of your life that makes you feel proud, now.

## Talent Is Not Enough

My friend, you can have the talent of a genius, but, if you're not able to remain committed to a path to achieve specific outcomes, you will lack the grit, the determination, and staying power necessary to win at the game you most want to win.

The depth of conviction in your heart toward a goal or change initiative defines the amount of staying power you will be able to muster on the journey toward the achievement of a goal. This conviction will be associated with a compelling vision, and a pleasure-pain association that impels you to think and believe, "I *must* do this."

Kenneth Blanchard asserts, "There's a difference between interest and commitment. When you're interested in doing something; you do it only when it's convenient. When you're committed to something, you accept no excuses; only results." These two perspectives provides clues to the level of passionate determination required to achieve most goals. A person whose mind is committed to a goal will demonstrate a passionate perseverance, even when faced with difficulty, on the path to accomplishing the goal.

## Honor the Struggle

Here's a fact of life. From one day to the next, you're not going to ALWAYS feel like doing everything it takes to achieve the success you want. Your personal habits will play a critical role toward the consistency of the actions you take toward your dreams and goals. When you maintain a state of BEing that's inner-directed, this mindset will inspire you to do whatever it takes to achieve the positive change you desire.

If you become outer-directed, your attention and energy will be focused more on what people think and believe about you and what you're doing. The need for validation is a distraction. Your consistency toward taking action will be like a yo-yo going up and down. The fickle feelings of people will dictate what you will do or won't do toward the achievement of your goals.

Honor the struggle. Growth and progress does not follow a straight line. Instead, you are presented with opportunities that will test your commitment to your vision. It is up to you to develop the ability to motivate yourself to maintain the excitement, passion, and sense of purpose associated with your goal in order to achieve it.

# Practice 7

# Be Driven by Discovery

*Curiosity adds zest in your life -*
*enriches your sense of security,*
*confidence, and well-being.*

*~Brian Grazer*

We are born curious. Think about the inquisitiveness of a 12 month old baby and a three year old toddler. They ask questions, over and over, about things around them that captivate their attention. As adults, we are often less fascinated by what they see. Their level of questioning can often be viewed by adults as an irritant. But, it is instinctive for babies and toddlers to be curious about the world around them. To them, everything in the world is new. For many adults, there's rarely anything in their everyday life that captivates their curiosity in this way. Be encouraged. The good news according to Brian Grazer author of *A Curious Mind*, "...no matter how much battering your curiosity has taken, it's standing by, ready to be awakened."

Curiosity urged me to register to attend Cape Fear Community College as a part-time student at the start of the New Year in 2000. After three years of trying to deny the harsh reality of the depth of my grief from the loss of my son Blease, I created and engaged in a daily sacred ritual which I practiced for a year to process the thoughts, feelings, and emotions associated with my grief.

This process liberated my soul from the unnecessary suffering I put myself through by denying the truth of my grief. It created such a big shift in my perspective and energy that my zeal and thirst for life inspired me to seek and seize new possibilities for me to grow and expand my network, skills and my service to the community of Wilmington, NC.

I enrolled in three classes: creative writing, public speaking, and intro to acting. I was on a fact finding mission. I wanted to gather information that could help me define a path for my speaking and writing aspirations. Out of the three classes, my acting class and the Buddhist professor teaching it literally opened up the world to me in ways I'd never experience because of the mindfulness training he taught us as a means for us to embody the character in the stories we were to portray when doing our acting scenes.

I kid you not, everything around me became more vibrant. The manner in which he taught mindfulness helped me become attune to sensory details in my surroundings. This skill enhanced my relationship with myself and others. Why? Because, it allowed me to to fully embrace the power of the present moment.

It helped me to quiet the chatter in my mind and embrace the stillness in my soul. I was more present in my interactions with people which improved my listening skills, and increased my influence as a leader. I was more at ease. From that point forward, I became a student of mindfulness and meditation practices.

One of his techniques for helping us enhance our observational skills involved each student visiting one of our favorite restaurants and observing the body language of patrons. Based on what we observed, we were expected to create characters and a narrative about what we perceived to have taken place in the scene at the restaurant. We were then expected to share what we observed in the restaurant with the class. This acting class remains in my top five of all my college coursework.

My curiosity about what might be possible if I pursued the speaking and writing aspirations in my heart led me to meet my Buddhist professor. He provided me the learning opportunity to explore what it feels like for my soul to embody the power of the present moment. He sparked my curiosity about mindfulness and meditation techniques.

The journey of developing my mindfulness and meditation practice has empowered me with the ability to quiet the chatter in my mind and embrace the stillness in my soul. My mindfulness and mediation practice continues to be life-affirming. I am a better person because of it. My life continues to be enriched because of my devotion to these practices.

**Be Open to Curiosity**

When was the last time you were curious about something to the point you took immediate action? How much more would you discover about yourself, the people in your life, and the world around you if you were more curious?

When you are driven by discovery, the eyes of your heart is open to seeing the world differently. It increases the likelihood that you will discover a newness about life that helps to expand your perspective and way of BEing in the world. But, you'll never know if this is a real possibility without becoming more curious about what you are truly capable of, and how much more you can enjoy the world, near and far.

Choosing to be driven by discovery is an act of bravery. Why? Because it requires you to move beyond what is familiar and embrace the unknown. To be honest, most of us to some extinct fear the unknown. There are moments when we would rather put up with the status quo because it provides us an illusion of security.

Here's a fact: every day you wake up, there are countless unknown scenarios that can occur in your life which you will have no control over. The ONE thing you have complete control over is how you choose to respond to them. That is it. Everything else can change without your consent. You may not like this truth. You may get pissed off at this truth, but, it doesn't change this truth.

## Link Pleasure to Curiosity

Facing the unknown is scary when the action we're considering to take is associated with pain. When we choose to associate pleasure with any action taken beyond our comfort zone, we increase our capacity to better manage our fears, doubts, and insecurities. When we face the unknown with a sense of self-trust, we feel a greater sense of certainty about our ability to manage unfamiliar situations.

Think about a moment when being curious resulted in you experiencing a positive outcome. Use your imagination and recall vivid details about the situation. Immerse yourself in the details of the situation using your senses. You are able to feel the pleasure experienced in this moment. Use this visualization to help you link pleasure to being curious about the unknown. This activity will help you cultivate a cognitive and emotional reference that can help you embrace curiosity as a tool to experience pleasure while broadening your horizons in life.

## Mindful Breathing Reduces Stress

I have included the following information because I understand how stepping into the unknown can initially be somewhat stressful. Practicing conscious breathing techniques will help reduce this stress.

In *Peace of Mindfulness* Barrie Davenport writes, "Conscious breathing reduces stress and promotes relaxation of the mind and body.

Slow, deep, rhythmic breathing causes a reflex stimulation of the parasympathetic nervous system, which results in a reduction in the heart rate and relaxation of the body." When you feel anxious about a new experience, center yourself with the following abdominal breathing exercise.

Breathing through your nose, push your stomach forward gently, and breathe through as though you are filling your stomach. When you exhale, breathe out slowly, and gently allow your stomach to return to its normal position. Abdominal breathing fills the lower lobes of the lungs, and it massages the abdominal organs by the movements of the diaphragm. This is a simple technique you can practice for a few minutes throughout the day to direct your focus back to the present moment with your breath while relaxing your body and managing stress.

## Curiosity Sparks Inspiration, Creativity and Innovation

In *The Curious Mind* Grazer writes, "Curiosity presumes that there might be something new out there.

Curiosity presumes that there might be something outside of our experience out there. Curiosity allows the possibility that the way we're doing it now isn't the only way, or even the best way."

When you adopt an inquisitive mind toward what else is possible in your life, your curiosity will spark ideas that can lead to fresh and better outcomes. When you take leaps, you are on a fact-finding mission of discovering what works and what doesn't work. Because you are resilient, you'll use failure as feedback to determine your next steps, either, move forward or axe the idea for a new one.

Curiosity will flame the fire in your soul with a belief that there is a new way, a better way to experience any aspect of your life. Your desire will prompt you to continue to take actions toward the possibilities you imagine.

## Curiosity + Building Leaders without Titles

After the one-on-one conversations I conducted with team members at the Fairfield Inn hotel about the employee opinion survey results, I gained an understanding of how they perceived me, and got a glimpse of who they aspired to be.

It became clear how I needed to show up for them as a leader. The information they'd shared about their aspirations peaked my curiosity. Could I develop a staff of leaders without titles and achieve a professional comeback?

During this time, *Oprah Winfrey's Book Club* was very popular. I decided to create a book club for our team. I used portions of the employee recognition budget and some of my bonus money to fund it for a year. From experience, books is an effective way to create a collective consciousness towards the achievement of goals.

My aim was simple and audacious: develop the leadership capacity of each team member. The hotel was structured with a general manager, assistant manager and two full-time supervisors. Everyone, except management, was an hourly employee. Each quarter, I chose a book that reinforced my perspective of them as leaders. During our monthly meetings, we would discussed key points from each book and how we could apply it in our work to improve our effectiveness as a team and the success of the hotel.

I hired a consultant to conduct a team building seminar so that each person would have a better understanding of how their role contributed to creating our team's success story. When the assistant manager relocated to Charlotte, NC, I decided that I wouldn't replace him with a new assistant manager right away.

I perceived this as opportunity to deepen my connection with team members and expand my reach of developing a staff of leaders without titles. I gave everyone raises and assigned each of them additional responsibilities. I was intentional about providing the staff with resources and a supportive environment that expanded their perspective of how they saw themselves, and what they believed about their capability toward building a winning team. This experiment provided me the autonomy to grow and develop the talents of each staff member. We were never the same as a result of this experiment. We were surprised by the level of success we were able to accomplish, especially considering our rocky start together.

One of the tests of our progress came when I shared with team members how I wanted our hotel to enhance our customer service experience for our VIP Fairfield Innsiders.

I wanted us to start turning down beds and placing refrigerators and welcome baskets in our VIP customer rooms upon arrival. I expected push back. Instead, I got more questions about 'how' we would make it happen instead of, "That's not what we do here." This meant to me that we had reached the point of connection and cohesiveness that would create opportunities for us to keep leveling up our customer service experience.

This idea was inspired by a combination of my experiences working within two other divisions of the company, Marriott's full-service and Courtyard division. In addition, I borrowed from Marriott's Residence Inn division and started conducting bi-weekly cook-outs for guests during the spring and summer months. All of this was happening in the mid-90s before these customer experiences became a norm for many limited-lodging hotel brands in the same category as the Fairfield Inn brand.

My commitment to investing in personal development and professional training for this staff, and hiring an assistant manager who had worked in several divisions of the company, enabled us to keep leveling up our customer service experience. This helped us to stand out in the mind of our customers, and in our market. We were able to maintain our market-share competitiveness even while newer hotels were being built around us, while securing business contracts that enabled us to maintain above average occupancy percentages in our market during the off season. This fact certainly helped us to maintain a stable staff.

By growing ourselves, we became a team that was able to grow the hotel's revenues and profits in ways that weren't expected and scoring high on customer service surveys, even during our hotel's five-year renovation. Curiosity as a leader helped me to discover and unleash the seeds of greatness of this staff which encouraged me to add it to my leadership toolbox with a knowing that it would serve me in the future.

## Trust Your Truth

Curiosity will help you break free of thoughts and beliefs entrenched in fear, doubt and insecurities. When you embrace curiosity with an open mind and open heart, your body will be infused with fresh energy. You will become hungry to learn and grow yourself. You wonder what else could be possible in a situation. You begin to take steps to play with the world to find out.

Be driven by discovery. Be open to the possibility of new possibilities. Instead of thinking and believing you have to control every aspect of your journey to experience your desired outcomes, be willing to trust and surrender to each moment as it unfold. You will be pleasantly surprised. Make feeling good a priority. Inhabit the energy of that which you desire, so that you radiate the energy and attract that which you seek to you. Remember to remember that your strong moments validate that you are enough. Trust in this liberating truth.

# Practice 8

# Brave the Way Forward

*Have the courage to follow your heart and intuition.*
*They somehow already know*
*what you truly want to become.*
~Steve Jobs

*What is Creative Living? Any Life that Is Driven More Strongly By Curiosity Than By Fear.*
*~Elizabeth Gilbert*

# The Brave New You Manifesto

## You Are Braver than You Believe.

Awaken to the Divine Within You.
Believe in Yourself. Trust that You Can Handle Life.
Self-Love and Bravery > Fear and Self-Doubt.
Face Your Fear while it is An Emotion,
Before It Becomes a Behavior.

## Be Intentional.

Get Clear About Your Core Desired Feelings.
Decide What You Stand For.
Decide What You Won't Stand For.
Open Your Heart and Mind to New Possibilities.
Connect and Collaborate with Braveheart People.

## Be Brave Every Day.

Be Grateful. Express Your Appreciation.
Be Still. Respect the Wisdom of Your Soul.
Be Kind. Respect Your Feelings
And the Feelings of Others.
Be Bold. Embrace New Possibilities with Enthusiasm.
Be Curious. Expand Your Comfort Zone.
Be the Hero or Heroine of Your Brave Story.

Braving your way forward is a multidimensional experience. You will need to reconnect with your authentic self to develop an unwavering trust in yourself, and in your ability to figure things out as level up your life. While you courageously pursue a path of building a foundation of self-trust grounded in a sense of *knowing* about the truth of your enoughness, who you are, what you stand for, where you are going and what it will take to get there, you will begin to empty yourself of patterns which no longer serve your present aspirations. The releasing of disempowering patterns will help you to lean into that which is sacred within yourself and life.

This process will inspire you to make new agreements with yourself and with life. Agreements that will liberate you, magnetize your energy, and increase your sense of personal power. You will no longer be willing to accept conventional wisdom as the be-all that so many people make it out to be. Instead, you will adopt a curious mind about what is possible and allow your sparks of intuition and creativity illuminate new paths forward. This state of liberation will without a doubt increase your joy and ability to thrive.

## Make Peace with Your Past

Every major breakthrough I've experienced has required me to embrace a "beginners mind" and "let go" of emotional interpretations of past experiences that were not serving my greater good. When I committed to doing the inner-work required to experience the release, my joy increased and I would gain greater clarity about next steps to optimize my present opportunities.

For example, recall the story that I shared about my fifth-grade solo singing performance and how my perception of my mom's lack of emotional support on that day resulted in me never really feeling comfortable receiving awards during my corporate career. Despite the amount of work that it took for me to be even considered for these awards, when I was recognized, I always felt awkward because I didn't want others to think that I was showing off. While writing this book, I came to realize for the first-time in my life that one of the reasons why I was able to follow the advice of not taking things personally was a result of the fact that mother's emotional detachment had enabled me to develop the ability to create an emotional distance when faced with numerous social situations and personal adversities.

This trait helped me to avoid a lot of peer pressure as a teen and adult. I was okay with not fitting in with the crowd and doing my own thing. This sense of autonomy provided me the freedom to explore. It often caused some people to perceive me as cold and aloof, while those who knew me personally and professionally knew that I was someone who could not only deliver results, and I had an uncanny ability to keep a calm demeanor in the midst of upheaval.

As I began to recall several pivotal moments in my life, I can now see how this trait influenced both my parenting and leadership style. I am certain it is one of the reasons why my daughter Dee is such a free thinker and has been able to maintain an unwavering resolve to build a successful business.

While editing this section of the book, tears began to swell up in my eyes and flow down my cheeks as I considered how I had once framed my mother's disposition as a child, and, after the process of healing my soul wound I experienced this paradigm shift about my mother's disposition. This perspective shift enlarged how my mother's emotional detachment had added so much value in all that I have and will accomplish in life beyond my fifth grade solo experience. This expanded perspective about my mother's emotional disposition feels liberating.

Making peace with our past requires us to do the work of releasing our attachment to emotional interpretations associated with past experiences we have deemed painful, and in some cases, unforgivable. I believe in the depth of my heart that when we truly want to experience freedom in our soul more than we want to be right about how we "see" a past experience, this state of mind and heart enables us to experience more empowering perspectives about our past.

This does not mean that you do not have a right to feel what you feel about a past experience. You do. Just know that you have the power to choose the meaning you attach to any experience. Accepting your truth can include releasing the emotional attachment to a past experience that continues to trigger you, or inhibit you from fully realizing your great potential. Mark Nepo states, "…our task in this life is to get out of the way as much as possible, so we might stretch into the power of unfiltered being, the way a small weed aches its way into the sun."

## Advance with Abandon

Brendon Burchard wrote in *The Motivation Manifesto,* "When our hearts yearn for action and growth, we should care little about what society says is possible or prudent. Let us judge for ourselves what is worth the risk. Let us decide what progress really means in life, as it surely means more than inching along like snails. Let us decide to take our first steps without knowing how the journey will turn out. If that defines us as reckless and crazy, then let us accept that fate and celebrate the fact that we shall not be cowards. Let us declare: *We Shall Advance with Abandon.*"

. Your ability to advance with abandon requires that you restore your faith in your spiritual power to create new models of reality. You just need an open mind and open heart to Spirit's guidance. Activating your spiritual power will always inspire your higher self to choose hope, faith, courage, and love. Instead of sitting on the sidelines dreaming about the life you want to live, you will advance with abandon toward living the life of your dreams.

I believe we are endowed with spiritual power when we are born because we are spiritual beings having a human experience on Earth. When our innate spiritual power is connected with love and faith in the Creator of the Universe which I believe to be God/Jesus/Spirit, and we surrender to the guidance and energy of Spirit working in and through us, our humility and surrendered heart enables us to activate a greater depth of spiritual power and authority.

A spiritual badass will make time to tune in to her inner-wisdom and tune out the noise of the world. She speaks words of life with authority. She steps boldly toward her destiny with humility and a belief that her steps are being ordered by a power greater than she or any human. She embraces forgiveness as a way of life. This practice activates her superpowers because it keeps her soul free of toxic emotions. She acknowledges that all persons on Earth have been created in the image of the Creator/God. Separation is an illusion. She understands that we are all One. She shows up in service to all on her journey to greatness.

## Step Boldly Toward Your Destiny

It is not enough for you to think you can be brave. You must live it. Only by living it, will you build the self-trust that is essential for you to step boldly toward a destiny of your own making. You actions will be the evidence that communicates to your higher self that you are ready and willing to embrace fear as a gift to show up, shine and succeed.

When you stand at the edge where fear ends and faith begins you are more likely to leap forward and soar. What edge is your faith summoning you to leap and soar beyond? The courageous wisdom in your heart will always encourage you to transform how you relate to fear. It knows that by shifting how you see fear, think about fear, and feel about fear, you will behave differently in the face of fear, which will expand your horizons in life.

Regardless of your motivation for reading this book, I can assure you that implementing the practices you have learned will help you create positive change in your life. And, it will help you differentiate yourself from the people around you. Why? Because a large portion of the people around you are allowing their overactive imagination consume them with fear, worry and anxiety. Individuals that demonstrate courage are usually perceived in a positive manner and viewed as leaders. Give yourself an advantage. In the face of your fears, initiate purposeful actions that contribute value in the lives of others while you manage and execute your plan to achieve your goals. You're going to be amazed by what begins to unfold in your life as you relate to fear as a gift!

Thank you for this opportunity to be your guide on this journey. Your next brave adventure awaits. The pursuit of your goals with soul will enable you to experience your most desired feeling states which will enrich your spiritual, mental, emotional and physical well-being. Make feeling good about yourself and your life a priority, not a second thought. You are deserving of all the good your heart is willing to receive. Open wide. The ongoing development of your self-leadership and emotional interdependence skills will empower you to *Find Your Brave* and embrace fear as a gift to show up, shine and succeed. You have it within you to be brave, be bold, and be badass. Go out and play with the world and prove it to yourself by taking on new adventures. You got this!

# Notes

## The Awakening

Nepo, Mark. (2011), *Finding Courage*, Conari Press.

## Practice 1 Dare to Desire

LaPorte, Danielle. (2014), *The Desire Map*, Sounds True, Inc.
Human Givens Theory, Human Givens Institute, Web.
Pressfield, Steven. (2012), *The War of Art*,
Black Irish Entertainment, Inc.
Brown, Brenė. (2012), *Daring Greatly*, Gotham Books

## Practice 2 Embrace Your Authentic Self

Covey, Stephen. (1989) *7 Habits of Highly Effective People*,
Simon & Schuster
Lakhiani, Vishen. (2016), *The Code Extraordinary Mind*,
 Rodale Inc.
Sadeghi, Habib, (2017), *The Clarity Cleanse,*
Grand Central Life & Style - Hachette Book Group
Warrell, Margie. (2015), *Brave*, John Wiley & Sons Australia, Ltd

## Chapter 3 You Are Enough

Dweck, Carol, (2007), *Mindset,* Ballantine Books
Buckingham, Marcus, (2009) *Find Your Strongest Life*,
One Thing Productions, Inc.
Nepo, Mark, (2014), *The Endless Practice*, Atria Paperbacks

# Notes

## Practice 4 Show Up for Yourself

Todd, Henry. (2013), *Die Empty*, Portfolio Penguin
Mohr, Tara, (2014), *Playing Big*, Penguin Books
Johnson, Whitney, (2016), *Disrupt Yourself*,
Taylor & Frances Group

## Practice 5 Disrupt Your Limits

Goldstein, Sam and Brooks, Robert. (2004) *The Power of Resilience*, McGraw-Hill

## Practice 7 Be Driven by Discovery

Davenport, Barrie, (2014), *Peace of Mindfulness*, Barrie Davenport
Grazer, Brian. (2015), *The Curious Mind*, Simon & Schuster

## Practice 8 Brave Your Way Forward

Burchard, Brendon. (2014). *The Motivation Manifesto,* Hay House

# About the Author

**Jackie Capers-Brown** is an award-winning corporate business leader. Today, she is the owner and CEO of Slay Your Greatness Academy, a personal development and leadership consultancy.

She is dedicated to helping individuals transform their relationship with fear in order to embrace the truth of their enoughness and embody the power of their authentic self to rise and slay their unique greatness in unique ways.

She's purpose driven and edgy. She's committed to empowering people to get out of their way and live true to themselves. For information about Jackie's coaching, training programs, speaker and consultant services, visit **www.jackiecapersbrown.com**.

## Connect with Jackie

Subscribe to Jackie's
"Level UP"
Bi-monthly Newsletter
Receive leading edge personal development and leadership strategies to level up your life, career and leadership success, plus other perks.

For more info, visit www.jackiecapersbrown.com

## Get Social with Jackie

www.facebook.com/SlayYourGreatnessAcademy
www.instagram.com/levelupwithjackiebrown
www.linkedin.com/jackiecapersbrown

## Book Review Request

Please share your thoughts about this book on the platform where you purchased it.

## Thank You

www.ingramcontent.com/pod-product-compliance
Lightning Source LLC
Chambersburg PA
CBHW071533220526
45469CB00003B/757